SABBATH
PRESENCE

SABBATH

APPRECIATING THE GIFTS OF EACH DAY

PRESENCE

KATHLEEN CASEY

ave maria press AmP Notre Dame, Indiana

www.avemariapress.com

ISBN-10 1-59471-068-6
ISBN-13 978-1-59471-068-1

Cover and text design by Brian C. Conley

Printed and bound in the United States of America.

Library of Congress Cataloging-in-Publication Data
Casey, Kathleen, 1960-
  Sabbath presence : appreciating the gifts of each day / Kathleen Casey.
    p. cm.
  Includes bibliographical references.
  ISBN-13: 978-1-59471-068-1 (pbk.)
  ISBN-10: 1-59471-068-6 (pbk.)
  1. Sunday. 2. Rest—Religious aspects—Christianity. 3. Sabbath. 4. Spiritual life—Christianity. I. Title.

BV111.3.C37 2006
263'.3—dc22
                                          2005027504

Contents

Introduction

In 1998 I was asked to form and lead a new committee for my parish. Our mission was to learn about the Jubilee values and then present them to the community. We had a year or so to educate ourselves about the Jubilee year and develop ways to incorporate those values into our parish life. We learned quickly that the Jubilee year was also referred to as the Sabbath of Sabbaths or a year of Sabbath for the Lord. The first task seemed obvious—find out about Sabbath. I knew the basics. The Sabbath was a day of rest called for by one of the commandments and the Jewish Sabbath was Friday evening to Saturday evening. That was the extent of my exposure to Sabbath. I looked up references to Sabbath in my trusty concordance, expecting to find a dozen verses I could study. I found more than a hundred direct statements about Sabbath and many more that referred to Sabbath by other names or phrases.

As I read and learned more, I started to see a pattern. Sabbath was called the sign of the covenant between God and his people. The practice of Sabbath concentrated on prayer, worship, and community. Sabbath was a time to appreciate all living things—human, animal, and vegetable. All of God's creation was to stop for a moment and ask, "To whom do I belong, to God or to the world?"

The pattern that emerged was simple: Sabbath is all about relationship. It's about a relationship with God, with others, with the created world, and with the inner self. Sabbath is first and foremost the sanctification of time, a time set apart to recognize and build an intimate relationship with God in all his manifestations. That relationship gives life and meaning to everything; without that relationship life has no meaning.

Viktor Frankl, a Jewish psychiatrist who survived the concentration camps of Nazi Germany, observed that the survivors of the camps were those who believed in a supreme being. They had faith in something greater than themselves. They had some relationship with God.

Today all the doing, achieving, accomplishing, and
acquiring is empty without a foundational relationship with
God. Those man-made things will pass away. A relationship
with God brings meaning to my life. As I studied, I quickly
began to understand why the practice of Sabbath was and is
so important.

Our parish committee found that the idea of Sabbath was
fundamental to the Jubilee itself, so we decided that it would
be the first value we would present to the parish. It also
seemed the most straightforward and the least likely to create
a controversy. It wasn't like we were asking people to give up
property or boycott paying mortgages. We were merely asking
people to recognize that a relationship with God periodically
deserved and required a step back from our busy lives to
refocus our priorities.

How hard could it be to encourage people to rest? How
hard could it be for them to stop for one day a week and
concentrate on their relationship with God and with each
other? We were going to give people permission to slow
down. We wanted people to take time to separate themselves
from the world, from culture, so they could listen to and
watch for God in their lives. What could be easier?

The group decided to ask the church staff to take the first
step and act as a model for the rest of the parish. The
committee approached the pastor with the idea that the staff
should designate one day a week as a Sabbath day. There
should be no church events, no meetings, no choir practice,
and no religious education—nothing on that designated day
each week (except Mass if Saturday or Sunday was the selected
day). It turned out to be more difficult than expected.

Looking at the calendar for the upcoming year, there
seemed to be no one day of the week that could be designated
as a Sabbath. Sundays were the only days for some religious
education classes, because every other day of the week was

scheduled to the brim with sports activities. Saturdays conflicted with many of the social activities and fund-raisers. Wednesdays were the only days for choir practice; Thursdays were the only days all the people on pastoral council could meet.

Every day was full. There was not one day that could be designated as our parish "day of the Lord." The church was truly a microcosm of the culture. The church didn't have time to step back from all it was "doing" in order to "be" with God. The church couldn't stop teaching religion long enough to practice Sabbath. The church couldn't stop talking about a relationship with God in order to have a relationship with God.

If the church itself could not practice Sabbath, knowing how important it was, then how could we expect our parishioners to do it? We finally were left presenting a watered down "idea" of Sabbath to the parish in the hopes that some individuals would be moved to set a little bit of time apart during the week to concentrate on their faith and families.

We presented the other Jubilee values to the parish in creative ways, but looking back I always felt that we missed an important opportunity. Our study of Sabbath sparked in me a longing to find a way to make time for God. It sounded so obvious that I should make time for God; I should have been hoping he would make time for me! I tried to do little things like not shopping on Sundays. I tried to set aside part of each day for prayer. I couldn't approach my family with some radical idea of complete rest on Sunday if I couldn't even incorporate a few small efforts into my own life. Many times I gave up the whole idea as just unrealistic, but then I would come across another verse or another spiritual book that talked about Sabbath. I couldn't seem to get away from it.

As I studied and prayed with these scriptures, God revealed to me the depth of the meaning of Sabbath. I discovered that Sabbath is multidimensional. Sabbath is not only an obligation, but it is also the embodiment of God's love. Scheduling and prioritizing a time to develop a relationship with God allows me to ask the bigger questions, such as:

- What are my values?
- Who am I?
- What is the meaning of life?
- Do I express my love and gratitude for family and friends?
- Who is my neighbor?
- Is my work fulfilling?

During the time I have set aside, I read scripture, look at the natural world, and get to know my God. These are questions and experiences that I don't usually make time for in my daily life.

When I do set time aside to notice God's presence, his grace becomes more evident each day. Sabbath is a gift of time to journey with God, to empty myself of past hurts and resentments. Sabbath is a gift of a new perspective, seeing God's creation afresh. Sabbath is a gift of time and space to appreciate the present moment before I'm off planning the next moment. Sabbath is a discipline that yields much fruit, but it also requires that I put less value on busyness and more value on being.

The Sabbath scriptures took me in many directions. I had to take a long hard look at my own life: my priorities, my calendar, my family, my community, and my inner self. I realized that Sabbath is not just about physical rest, it's about relationships with God and with the people and things he loves. Each aspect of Sabbath I explored ended in the same place, with God's greatest gift of all, with the realization that God is always loyal to his covenant of love. It is I who must actively accept the gift of love and practice my part of the relationship. I'm relieved that God obviously tries to make it easy for me. He's always available, always ready to take me back when I forget him, and always ready to forgive when I put other things in his place. All I have to do is be open to receive. I have to put myself in a time and place where I can be receptive to God's gifts. I read somewhere that 90 percent of prayer is just showing up. Prayer, Sabbath, and a relationship with God are all the same in that respect—90 percent of it is just showing up to receive the gifts.

I hope that these reflections on Sabbath will encourage you to evaluate your relationship with God, with yourself, with others, and with the world. I hope the scriptures will inspire you, as they did me, to look closely at your calendar, your checkbook, and the use of your time. I do not pretend that this is a presentation of my many years of experience with keeping the Sabbath. It's really quite the opposite. Like so many others, I have not had a family tradition of truly keeping the Sabbath. Instead, this is more about my struggle to incorporate some Sabbath time into each day and to carve out a special time each week to be with God. It is about the gifts I have received when, in some way, I've made an effort to be in the presence of God. Journey with me on this expedition and discover the many gifts that God gives us when we celebrate his presence through the practice of Sabbath.

1

The Gift of Emptying

> During the seventh year the land shall have a complete rest, a sabbath for the LORD, when you may neither sow your field nor prune your vineyard.
>
> —LEVITICUS 25:4

In her book *Everyday Sacred*, Sue Bender retells the story of a student who makes a pilgrimage to see a famous monk. He travels a very long way seeking wisdom. When he arrives he starts asking very profound questions but is frustrated because the monk offers no answers. Seeing that the student is upset, the monk instructs him to pour himself a cup of tea. He says, "I will tell you when to stop pouring." The student pours and pours and pours until the cup starts spilling over but still the monk does not tell him to stop. The student protests, saying, "The cup is too full; it can't hold any more!" The monk replies, "And so it is with you."

The student could not hear the answers to his questions. He could not find the wisdom he sought because he was already too full of many things. Only when we are empty will there be room for the spirit.

The vessel that symbolizes my life is my old coffee cup. It's stained from use; it's been full and empty. The contents have often been spilled and at times it has sat for hours after I've forgotten what's in it. So often the cup of my life is full from doing many things. But with that fullness—and often it is a good fullness (I am privileged to have so many people and things I care about)—comes the reality that there is not room for anything else. Sometimes there is not room for me, my family, or God. Those are the times I become aware that my life is so cluttered that I cannot listen attentively to the spirit.

Years ago I went on a silent retreat. It was five days in complete silence except for a brief meeting once a day with a spiritual director. For the first couple of days I thought I'd go crazy—there were a lot of things that I needed to do and I felt like I was wasting my time while things just piled up at home. I felt guilty for not accomplishing anything. By the third day I resigned myself to the fact that the world would continue to revolve without me, people would solve their own problems, and all those things on my "to do" list would either be there when I got back, or better yet, they might be taken care of by someone else. I was finally able to let go of all the things I was worried about, and realized that I had nothing to do—absolutely nothing. And I didn't know what to do with myself. I thought, "There must be someone who needs me to make coffee or set up chairs or fix something." But nobody needed me to do anything. In fact I wasn't even allowed to ask if I could be of assistance.

I could not give anything; I was there to relax and reflect and I felt empty. I felt impoverished. It was a scary feeling at first. Who was I if I wasn't the helper, the leader, or the planner?

Slowly, I learned to appreciate the emptiness. It became a good kind of poverty. Finally I could lie in the grass, look up at the clouds, and listen, just listen. I prayed a different kind of prayer that week—I felt that just being in the presence of God was enough. It's one of those close-to-God moments that I will never forget. It still amazes me that it took me so long to empty myself so I could start to be filled. It's something I would love to do again. Since then I have found that I can have moments like that every day. And if I really try I can actually have a whole day.

Retreats are often the only times when we can really break away. Most of us need a change of scenery, a forced exile, before we can really let go. Too often we can be like the monk's tea cup: full of many things (good and bad), especially if there hasn't been time to do any emptying recently. Our cup may not just be full of our current responsibilities and worries; it can also carry our past. In *The Power of Now*, Eckhart Tolle talks about our hurts, resentments, pains, judgments, betrayals—all are gathered and stored on a cellular level called "the pain body." If these troubles go unchecked, we then react out of the pain body, not out of our true selves. We can be totally unaware of it, and usually are. At that point, we don't possess painful memories; the pain body possesses us. A psychologist friend of mine said it this way: people don't overreact, they just aren't aware of what they are really reacting to.

Tolle tells about a cycle of possession where the pain body becomes our identity. A friend of mine who has a child with Attention Deficit Disorder says that they are an "ADD family." The disorder has become part of the identity of the family. I ask the students I teach to refer to a patient by name and only then add that they had a stroke, for example, instead of referring to them as "the stroke patient in room 220." It may seem like a minor issue but I think it's important that my interns see the person first, not the disorder. When the pain body becomes part of our identity we start to define ourselves by our illness, past or current abuse, resentments, or other negative feelings that we might not want to deal with. It becomes part of our mask, or the role we play, which is called the false self. Many psychologists say that discovering and detaching from the false self is the hardest spiritual and psychological work. That is the work of emptying.

It is said that the desert fathers retreated to the desert to discover two things. They went to find what they should let go of and what they should hold on to. In other words, what they should ignore and what they should love. The first lesson of the desert was to ignore the praises and the insults of other people and the feeling of worthiness obtained through the opinion of others. Only then could they learn the second lesson, which was to find what they would love. If they were not motivated by the opinion of others or the culture then what would they give their life to?

The desert was seen as a place of temptation, but it is a place where we must all go to meet the devil that is ourselves. Jesus went to the desert, where he physically emptied himself by fasting. There he faced temptation. He faced the temptation to *accomplish* by making stone into bread. He faced the temptation of *prestige* when Satan dared him to throw himself off the mountain to prove that God's favor would protect him. He faced the temptation of *security* through worldly possessions when Satan offered him the kingdoms of the world. These are temptations of all mankind. These are demons of the false self.

Modern psychologists describe the desert of the early Christian mystics as a laboratory for dealing with the ego, or the false self. In the desert there are no distractions, so we are forced to deal with our anxieties, our need for affirmation, control, and security. The desert doesn't care about our need for comfort or solace, or about our identity or worthiness, and that makes it a perfect place to deal with the problem of the ego.

The monks, like Jesus, went to the emptiness of the desert to face their false self and detach from the pain and illusions of the self and the world. It is then that the monks learned about love—a selfless, unconditional love. They emptied themselves in the desert so they could be filled with the love of God. In his book *Merton's Palace of Nowhere*, James Finley summarizes Merton, saying:

> We can only hope to create that empty space, that context for insight in which the unexpected everything can rise mysteriously and effortlessly out of nothingness in which we wait for God.

After meditating on scripture or spiritual writing I find it helpful to journal about it. The technique I use when journaling is to write while trying not to think. I write anything that comes to me without analyzing or editing. Sometimes when I am able to journal that way, I end up writing a dialogue between my conscious mind and my subconscious or the spirit within me. The following is one such dialogue after I read Finley's statement about emptiness.

Maybe my attraction to Sabbath is an intuitive need to be connected with God and I know that must come first out of emptiness. If I have too much to do or say or think about, I can't sit and listen. It is a spiritual discipline that intellectually I know is necessary. But how do I create such a place, openness to You?

Practice.

Practice what exactly? Where do I go, what do I do?

Nowhere, nothing.

That's very hard. I'd much rather try to see you in things and in people—that I can do— but in nothing, how do I recognize you?

With other eyes, inner eyes will see. Let go of the senses and the knowledge; let go of seeking some new insight or new bit of understanding. Your effort to find one new thing blocks your way to finding all things new.

Easier said than done. You gave me a brain and senses and now you don't want me to use them?

I gave you other things, too, but you haven't used them as much so you don't know how. They are gifts no less important but harder to practice. They don't come as naturally in your busy world. Explore the gifts that are hidden in plain sight; but you can't do that until you empty yourself of all other things. You are your biggest obstacle— the you as you define yourself. Empty yourself of those judgments and needs. That in itself is a gift.

FOR MEDITATION:

Choose a vessel as a symbol of your life and spirit right now. First, fill your vessel (how full is up to you). Then look at it. Let it speak to you. Look into your vessel—what things are there?

How can this vessel be a metaphor for you? What is significant about it?

What things have been there for a long time (all the things you do, past successes and failures, hurts, offenses, joys, and sufferings)? What is unused but still remains?

What things are in the vessel that don't belong to you and should be somewhere else?

What things should have been removed from your vessel but instead have been kept?

- Have there been times that I have felt so stressed, cluttered, or hurt that I felt out of control?
- Are there times when I reacted out of the pain body? When does that happen and how does it feel?
- Do I need emptying—physical or psychological or both?
- How can I allow myself to be emptied?

FOR DISCUSSION OR JOURNALING:

Describe a time when you felt empty and ready to be filled.

FOR THE WEEK AHEAD:

Put a bowl or cup on your table and fill it. In the evening, sit for a few minutes and reflect on your day. Examine what is in your vessel. Give your day and all it contains back to God and then empty your vessel.

"God touches us with a touch that is emptiness and empties us."

—THOMAS MERTON

2

The Gift of Being

You must also tell the Israelites: Take care to keep my sabbaths, for that is to be the token between you and me throughout the generations, to show that it is I, the LORD, who make you holy.

—EXODUS 31:13 (NAB)

One of the most significant gifts of Sabbath is that it gives me the opportunity to reorient myself in the world. The practice of Sabbath takes me out of the culture of doing so I can recognize the many false gods in the world. On that day I am commanded to be still and remember that only God is God (Ps 46:10). According to law, Jews could not do anything on the Sabbath that affected the world. They could not make any creative or destructive change in the world. For that day they acknowledged that all power comes from God. They were given the freedom to acknowledge their place as a creation of God.

The Hebrew scriptures say that idols are substitutes for the divine presence. It is easy to look back at the story of God's people wandering in the desert and recognize that the golden calf was an idol. The Israelites hoped that praying and giving sacrifices to the golden calf would lead them out of the endless desolation of the desert. Idols promise control over a scary and chaotic world. We still have our idols today, but they take less obvious forms. Modern technology and the human mind seem to offer that to us today. For example, I feel more secure and in control of my life if I have my cell phone. With new discoveries every day, we think that modern science can understand and explain all the world's mysteries. But technology is a false god just like the golden calf. It gives us an illusion of security and control. The gods of our culture are difficult taskmasters because they lure us into the illusion that we can be the master of our own universe. Saint Bernard of Clairvaux said, "Those refusing to be ruled by God's gentleness will have the misfortune of being ruled by their own selves. . . ."

I have a friend who is in a twelve-step program. She told me that the first step is to acknowledge her powerlessness and the second is to believe that a power greater than herself, a supreme being, can restore her life. The "Serenity Prayer" that starts each meeting reminds them of those first crucial steps.

> God grant me the serenity to accept the things
> I cannot change, the courage to change the
> things I can and the wisdom to know the
> difference.

This could very well be a Sabbath prayer, because Sabbath works in practice what this prayer and the first steps of the program describe in words. My friend says that it is important to go to meetings, even after years of sobriety, to remember her powerlessness and to renew her hope in a God who loves her. In a way, Sabbath does that for me. By "not doing" on the Sabbath, I remind myself that I am not the one in charge. It reminds me of my powerlessness; it reminds me that I am not God and neither is an institution, a particular value, or a person. God endowed us with free will, so we wield a great deal of power over our world. Our culture puts such an emphasis on our ability to affect the world economically, environmentally, and militarily that it's easy to forget that the freedom and power we enjoy were given by the ultimate power. My friend says she's been working on those first steps of the program for years and will probably continue to work on them for the rest of her life. She says it's something you just have to keep learning. Sabbath keeps me coming back to the same reality, that only God is God, and there is hope and relief in that fact. I suspect that I, too, will work on this for the rest of my life.

It is important for us to stop work and to remember the originator of all creative work for another reason. In this society I have learned to judge others and myself by the effects of my work. When I introduce myself to someone, I say that I'm a therapist, a mother, a wife, and sometimes where I went to school or where I work. I tell them what I do. I would venture to say that most of us think of ourselves in terms of what we do, what we produce, or what we have achieved.

My son came home from his first day at school and one of the "get to know you" exercises for his class was to share what they wanted to "be" when they grew up. He told me that he and his fellow students wanted to be doctors, veterinarians, businessmen, and teachers, to name a few. Of course those are all things we *do*.

Today our natural stance is not empathetic or compassionate; culturally our stance is comparative and competitive. I distinguish myself by comparing myself to others. Going through the college application process with my daughter made this idea more obvious. On each application she had to not only give her grade point average and standardized test scores, but also most of the essays asked her to say why she was a better candidate than her fellow classmates. We are taught early in life to describe ourselves and identify ourselves by what we *do* instead of who we *are*.

This idea can be very powerful when what we do is service-oriented, because our values as Christians tell us to do good for others. It's the age-old conflict between James and Paul. Paul would warn that salvation is a gift that can't be earned with good works. James would agree but add that faith is empty without the expression of that faith, which is service to others.

Sabbath allows me to live in both worlds. I can express my gratitude for God's many gifts by daily serving others. But for one day I can discipline myself not to work—even in service—so I can realize in heart, mind, body, and soul that I only serve because God gave the gifts. I am merely a steward of those gifts. On that one day I cannot be identified by what I do. On that day it is clear that my identity is who I am, and that is, simply, a child of God.

This idea of being, as opposed to doing, is so foreign to our culture that I wanted to think of an example of someone who is good at just being. It's a powerful statement that my best example is an infant, who hasn't had the time or opportunity to judge himself and build up an identity or walls or masks. The infants in our medical unit are a wonderful image of being. They receive and trust perfectly, without question or comment, and they give back without even being aware of it. They don't ask if they deserve to be cared for, fed, or loved. They don't need to reciprocate. They don't need to justify or explain their dignity or worth.

In one case, our roles were reversed. All of us on the team had to learn how to just be there for one of our infants. Sara was born very prematurely at just over a pound. She spent more than six months in our unit. Her parents had detached from her almost as soon as she was born, which made us her family more than anyone else.

As medical caregivers we are trained to solve problems. Even our notes are "problem based." There is a list of problems involving every system of the body. The problem and the medical course of action are charted every day on every patient. When we review the case with other staff members we naturally refer to each problem and its possible solution. Unfortunately, after months of treatments, procedures, tests, and therapy, Sara was dying. There was nothing more that could be done.

During her last day she was swollen and discolored. Each person who had taken care of her, and especially the nurses who had spent so many hours with her, were given a final gift. We were given some time to just be with Sara. As I held her for the last time she tried so hard to smile and to open her eyes. I felt helpless, but it was good for me to just hold her and be with her. The nurses who had loved her and cared for her held her for hours. Sara loved us, not because of what we could do for her, but just for being present. Everything else stopped that day. All the business, all the energy and movement, stopped around that crib. No amount of doing could help. In the end the best thing we could do for her was to do nothing at all. It was a sad and humbling experience, and at the same time it was peaceful and reassuring; Sara would be in the hands of the God who made her. Her dignity came not from what she could do or in the promise of future achievement. She was holy because God made her holy, as he makes each of us holy.

I can say and know intellectually that I am more than the sum total of what I do, but it is much harder to really believe it. Thomas Merton suggests that to avoid the trap of identifying ourselves by what we do, we must be detached from our deeds and be attached to God's presence. It is only through his presence in us that we do good things. Jesus said it this way, when he answered the young man who addressed him as "good master," "Why do you call me good? No one is good but God alone" (Lk 18:19).

Our society values work and achievement above all else; my God values me. In my environment, it is difficult to maintain my status as a human *being* instead of a human *doing*. I'm not condemning the good works that we do out of compassion and love. But it is all too easy to start believing we are what we do, and that is an illusion. Henri Nouwen says, "In solitude we can listen to the voice of the One who spoke to us before we could speak a word, who healed us before we could make any gesture to help, who set us free long before we could free others, and who loved us long before we could love anyone." These are God's gifts, but they are only viable when they are born of an intimate relationship with God.

> That evening, at sundown, they brought to him all who were sick or possessed with demons. And the whole city was gathered around the door. And he cured many who were sick with various diseases, and cast out many demons; and he would not permit the

> demons to speak, because they knew him. In
> the morning, while it was still very dark, he
> got up and went out to a deserted place, and
> there he prayed (Mk 1:32–35).

In the midst of all this activity of healing, preaching, and moving from town to town, Jesus went apart to pray. Jesus separated himself from the people, from his work, and even from his friends, so he could have some quiet time with God. He went to a solitary place to be alone with his father. He who was healer, teacher, and savior left those roles behind to remember that he was the Son of God. Jesus recognized his need to step back and realign himself with the core of his being. Jesus counseled the disciples to do the same. "He said to them, 'Come away to a deserted place all by yourselves and rest a while.' For many were coming and going, and they had no leisure even to eat" (Mk 6:31).

Jesus and his disciples needed to break away from the crowd and go off to the desert, to a quiet place so they could listen to God. They needed an environment that made listening possible. I feel a need to be obedient to the practice of Sabbath because it is like that quiet environment. Sabbath is like that desert experience. It is an empty place. It is a place set apart from the busyness of my daily world; one that takes me out of my cultural world. It is a place of *not* doing. Sabbath is that still point where I am forbidden to do. Sabbath doesn't allow me to do or to accomplish. The psychological and cultural detachment must be made between who I am and what I do. My overidentification with the things I do creates a false self or mask of who I am. When I do as Jesus commanded, "Go into your room and shut the door and pray to your Father who is in secret" (Mt. 6:6), I can then let go of the false self, and God can help me discover who I truly am.

We are all like the Sabbath. We have been sanctified by God, not because of what we do, but because of the one who made us holy. Sabbath isn't a relationship with God, but it does put me in a more conducive environment to be attentive to the relationship that already exists. Initially, it may only be an outward practice of not doing; it may be like wandering around in the desert. Eventually that wandering opens up a place where I can truly listen to God. Without first listening deeply to that inner authority of the spirit, I cannot develop the discernment I need to know when and where God directs me to serve. Without first listening to God who says, "It is I . . . who make you holy," I cannot recognize that holiness in myself or in others.

"Be still and know that I am God."

—PSALM 46:10

FOR MEDITATION:

Nature is a good example of "just being." Thomas Merton said the best thing about praying in nature is that everything around you is doing the perfect will of God; you just have to fit in. Notice the trees, grass, and sky. Just be with God's creation as one of God's creatures. How does it feel?

- What does "I, the LORD, sanctify you" mean to me?
- Do I have a difficult time "just being"? Why?
- Do I attach any judgments about myself or others when there is no "productive" activity?

FOR DISCUSSION OR JOURNALING:

Share a time when you could just "be" with God. How did that feel?

"Religion has largely to do with doing, spirituality has to do with being."

—FRANK TUOTI,
WHY NOT BE A MYSTIC

3

The Gift of Balance

God saw everything that he had made, and indeed, it was very good. And there was evening and there was morning, the sixth day.

Thus the heavens and the earth were finished, and all their multitude. And on the seventh day God finished the work that he had done, and he rested on the seventh day from all the work that he had done. So God blessed the seventh day and hallowed it, because on it God rested from all the work that he had done in creation.

—GENESIS 1:31–2:3

I was brought up hearing the first Creation story in Genesis, but recently I noticed something new in the story. I noticed the balance that was created. God created light and dark, water and dry land, day and night, male and female, and, finally, the work of creation was balanced with rest. Our society values work. We are valuable because of what we produce and what we can buy. In our society work is certainly considered good. In the Genesis story, God also said that the work of creation was good. Notice that when he spoke of the Sabbath he did not say "it is good;" it says God "hallowed it." He made the Sabbath holy, which means "to make whole." Rest makes the work of creation "whole." Rest is holy when it balances work, and work is not complete until it is balanced by rest. Creation was not complete or holy until there was the Sabbath rest.

Rest is not the same as leisure activities, hobbies, or pastimes; those are still doing things. The Bible doesn't say that God rested on the seventh day by working on his sailboat. Many of us keep doing more and more leisure activities to escape from our everyday lives or in an effort to gain balance. These efforts are ineffective because they do not offer true rest. Have you ever felt like you need a couple of days to recoup from your busy weekend or from a hectic vacation? That kind of "rest" isn't refreshing or satisfying to the spirit. It doesn't give balance because it's still work; it's just a different kind of work.

The babies in our neonatal intensive care unit need a lot of rest to help them grow. It's humbling to watch a tiny baby, not much more than a pound, attached to wires and tubes, fighting to live. Their skin is so thin that veins and bones can be seen. They look even more fragile than they actually are. They have no fat and no ability to maintain their body temperature, so even keeping warm is hard work. When they are taken out of their protected environment and placed on the parent's chest, skin to skin, the parents are very nervous that the baby will get cold. They're worried that the baby will destabilize from too much exposure. But instead, the parent's body adjusts its temperature to keep the baby warm, and the baby's heart rate, respiratory rate, blood oxygen level, and temperature all stabilize. Their bodies become one in perfect balance. The child typically falls into a deep, quiet sleep and sometimes the parent does too. It is obvious that our bodies harmonize and balance internally, with other people and with our environment. When we can find that internal and external balance, we can find rest. We need darkness and light, sea and dry land, male and female, work and rest. Like those infants, we need the silence of the Sabbath rest to balance the noisy activity of our day-to-day world.

Scripture is full of opposites—things that balance each other. The story of Martha and Mary is a story of balance. One woman felt the need to work, while the other felt called to sit and listen at the feet of Jesus. Jesus calls his disciples to ministry and to prayer.

The contradictions among the writings of the Christian scriptures may cause difficulty for some readers, but for me one version of the story gives balance to another and often enhances the meaning. For example, in Paul's letters he describes the Holy Spirit most often as active within the community, the body of Christ. In John's gospel, the Paraclete (his word for the Spirit) is most active in the individual. Neither description is wrong or more right. In fact, reading them both and assimilating them both into my image of the Spirit gives me a fuller understanding of the action of the Spirit in my life. I know that I have felt the Spirit during my prayer time, but there have also been times that I am acutely aware of the Spirit during a moving liturgy with the community.

The early church, inspired by the Spirit, chose four different accounts of the life and message of Jesus. Historians, linguists, and theologians have spent countless hours trying to determine the most accurate account. But treasuring only one account would have shown us an incomplete Savior. When taken together, the four gospels, with their contradictions and repetitions, give a fuller picture of Jesus and his message.

Our faith is full of things that, on the surface, oppose each other but in fact create a balance. We believe in a God who is totally other than ourselves but is our most inner self. Jesus is fully human and fully divine. We have an image of a God who is omnipotent, invisible, and intangible and another image of God in Jesus who is palpable and corporeal when he is hanging, tortured and bleeding, on a cross. Both images must be held and assimilated by the Christian mind and faith. The extremes give texture, meaning, and balance. The extremes challenge us to look further.

We are all made up of contradictions and opposites. Hopefully some of those extremes balance out our character and our lifestyle. Each of us is called to be balanced, complete beings. We are called to holiness as individuals. God said, "You shall be holy, for I the LORD your God am holy" (Lev 19:2). God is holy and complete and we are made in that image. God created opposites in the world and in us. We, too, are made of opposites. We, too, have our light side and our dark side, our gifts and our flaws.

To gain balance we must acknowledge both our light and our dark. Some of us find it easy to name our gifts, talents, and strengths; for others it is easier to list our faults and weaknesses. The balance comes with recognizing that both are a part of us. The challenge of our light side is the responsibility to share those gifts, talents, and strengths with others.

A man I knew realized that his gift was making money, but he judged making money as only a necessary evil in the world. He never considered managing money as a gift. Money management just didn't sound very religious, so it took him years to realize his gift. He thought that being a volunteer for things like Habitat for Humanity and the grounds ministry at church seemed more valuable, but he had no talent for manual labor. When he finally recognized his true gifts he could then use them to help those in his community. He joined the board of a nonprofit organization and helped them become very successful in raising and managing their money, thereby allowing the organization to help many more people. What he once thought of as his dark side was really a wonderful talent—a light for others.

At a workshop, I was asked to identify my weaknesses. What I came up with were just my little irritating bad habits, but those are not really my dark side. It took much longer for me to recognize the dark part of myself. We were told that we might find our dark side by noticing when we had an immediate negative reaction to someone or something. That reaction is a hint, because the characteristics we don't like in ourselves are often the irritating characteristics we immediately recognize in another person. Jesus tells us to do the same when he asks, "Why do you see the speck in your neighbor's eye, but do not notice the log in your own eye?" (Mt 7:3).

The psychologist Karl Jung would call our dark side our shadow self. The shadow is that part of us which we keep hidden, especially from ourselves. When we remain unaware of our shadow side, we are living in denial and imbalance, because the shadow is also who we are. When we recognize the shadow, it can even be a gift.

Learning the Enneagram, a personality typology, helped me discover my shadow. I'm a personality type that the Enneagram calls the Avenger (or the Defender). When I read the description of that type I knew that person could not be me. I heard words like intimidating, aggressive, "lovable bulldozer"; obviously not me. It took me two years to examine myself and, with the help of some dear friends, I came to accept those traits as part of my personality. Since then, I've been able to catch my shadow self in the act. Sometimes I can even temper that energy so my defense of a principle doesn't bulldoze some innocent bystander. When I was growing up, my family moved around a lot. Being an introvert made it difficult for me to enter a new school every few years. I have learned that my tendency to be introverted is balanced by my passion to get involved in any cause. Instead of fighting or denying those characteristics, now I am grateful for them.

Sabbath is like the center of a seesaw. It is a still point in the middle of my life that allows me to balance the many aspects of my self and my life. For six days out of seven I look outward. I look out toward my patients, my children, my spouse, and my parish community. My days are filled with endless projects, chores, jobs, and diversions. The practice of the Sabbath rest on the seventh day of my week separates me from the culture of stimulation and busyness and gives me a moment to look inside, to reconnect and re-create balance within myself.

I find it worthwhile to examine all the aspects of life periodically to see if my life is in balance. I divide my life into different categories: spiritual, physical, intellectual, family, work, hobbies, social, and financial. Then I list the things that I do to focus on each part of my life. I determine how much time I spend in each area, each week. If my waking hours during the week add up to 112 hours, I can quickly see if my life is balanced. For example, I spend about forty hours a week at work, including my commuting time, fifteen hours doing work for church committees, and fifteen hours doing chores at home. I spend about fourteen hours a week with my children and seven to ten hours in prayer. When I map out my life in this way, my weak areas (such as exercise time) pop out at me and I try to spend some extra time in that area of my life.

Another way we can examine those same aspects of our lives is by separating the things that are external in nature from the things that are internal (physical exercise versus prayer, for example). Another approach is to divide the categories into activities that build our energy and activities that deplete it. In this way we can see if our lives are balanced between work and rest and between the internal and external self, work and family, etc. Whichever method you choose to examine these aspects of your life, the process can help you better plan and live the balanced life to which God calls you.

For Meditation

- What things in my personality do I not like to see or accept?
- What parts of my dark side, my shadow, may actually become strengths—my golden shadow or light side?
- Do I find it more difficult to accept compliments or criticism?
- What are my shadow characteristics?
- Do I feel my life is balanced? Why or why not? How could I become more balanced?

For Discussion or Journaling:

Describe a time when you had to face your shadow. How did it feel? How did it affect you?

Describe a time when you felt your life was completely balanced, and another time when it was imbalanced.

"**J**esus, help me balance the active and the quiet aspects of my life, recognizing both as a way of prayer."
—MARY VAN BALEN HOLT,
A DWELLING PLACE WITHIN

4

The Gift of Boundaries

You shall keep the sabbath, because it
is holy for you; everyone who profanes
it shall be put to death; whoever does
any work on it shall be cut off from
among the people.

—EXODUS 31:14

The Hebrews protected the time of Sabbath with many rules and regulations and with very severe penalties. There are more than 200 chapters in the books of Jewish laws that regulate the Sabbath. The Hebrews put boundaries around the Sabbath to keep it holy. There were thirty-nine specifically prohibited activities and each of them had subdivisions. For example, they could eat, but they were not permitted to cook; nor could they carry anything beyond the walls of their home. They could not tie permanent knots but could tie shoelaces; they could not begin or complete any useful activity. Some said that even to plan a project mentally was a violation. In the end the laws excluded almost every human activity.

The restrictions were complicated and may seem superfluous to us today, but there was good reasoning behind them. God gave man dominion over the things of the earth and for six days man imposed his will on the earth, but on the Sabbath man had to remember that his ability to effect change in the world was given as a gift from the one true God. For that day they relinquished mastery over the world and remembered God's mastery over all. On that day the Hebrews recognized their limits. It is just as important for us today to remember that we are creature and not creator, like the Hebrews who protected the Sabbath at all costs.

When I was in college I resolved to read the Bible cover to cover. I did pretty well until I got to Leviticus. The first couple of books were full of the biblical stories I remembered from my childhood. They were exciting and colorful stories. But when I came to Leviticus it was full of rules and regulations. I couldn't imagine why this was chosen as scripture. How could verse after verse of tedious detail bring us closer to God? But this book was part of the foundation of the fledgling society of Israel.

Many scholars report that when Moses brought the slaves out of Egypt, the trip to the Promised Land should have taken less than two weeks. But the people could not just "walk humbly with [their] God" (Micah 6:8). Instead, it took forty years to mold them into a people of God. I think God would have been pleased with the simple covenant: "You will be my people and I will be your God." But the people were demanding and defiant. Boundaries had to be put in place to help them. Moses began by giving them ten simple laws, directly from the mouth of God. The commandments were clearly stated and seemed fairly simple to follow. They didn't appear to need further explanation.

The third law was to keep holy the Sabbath. Moses didn't need to give a dissertation on the relationship between man and the universe or a higher being; it was God's command, and that should have been enough. People being people, it was not enough. They stretched, broke, and bent the law; therefore, more specific laws, practices, regulations, and penalties were developed, which brings me right back to Leviticus. I think my experiences as a parent help me understand that book better now.

Unfortunately I see myself in the wayward people of Israel. I, too, should be able to walk humbly with my God but continually choose to go my own way. When I was a child, my parents would tell me not to walk across the street alone. To me it was merely a restriction of my freedom. I would argue and ask why. My father's favorite explanation was "Because I said so." As I grew up, my mother began to explain why they developed the rules of the house. It often had a lot to do with keeping track of so many children. I think my father always saw us as his very vulnerable children and so he continued to say "Because I said so," regardless of our age or maturity.

I remember promising myself never to say that to my children. Years later I found myself trying to explain the dangers of electricity to my two-year-old as she tried sticking her hair clip into a light socket. As she persisted in asking me why, I finally succumbed and said, "Because I said so!" At that moment, I needed to give her firmer boundaries, not further explanations. She couldn't handle the freedom of choice until she first knew the limits.

Being a therapist in a neonatal intensive care unit allows me to observe and learn from the premature babies (preemies) I treat. One of the fundamentals that we as caregivers must accommodate is the infant's innate need for boundaries. Our preemies are nested with a blanket roll on all sides because they have no sense of homeostasis (where they are in space). They need to be able to feel and push against soft boundaries so they can work their muscles, orient themselves in space, and feel secure. Some people don't understand this fundamental need. If a baby looks sleepy while he is being fed, the caregiver might unwrap the blankets and sometimes tickle the baby's feet in hopes of waking him. Instead, the baby will often startle; his arms, hands, and legs will extend or reach out in panic. These are signs of stress. The baby is communicating that something is not right. He is also reaching for boundaries to reestablish his security.

As babies grow they still search for boundaries. If they are denied the soft boundaries of the swaddled blanket they will creep and move until their head or feet find the hard, unforgiving boundaries of the bassinet or crib. Only when babies have a secure position within boundaries do they explore and develop mature movement patterns. The boundaries are needed to help them orient themselves; from there they can begin to grow outward and to interact with a new world.

This pattern of seeking boundaries holds true as we mature. When my teenager was anticipating going off to college she would get indignant with me about all the "unfair" restrictions I put on her life. She protested any perceived threat to her independence. Her favorite line was "I can't wait until I'm completely on my own, then you won't be checking up on me all the time." But every night she stopped in my room on her way to bed and said, "Don't forget to come and kiss me goodnight." She couldn't kiss me goodnight right there in my room; she wanted that dependable routine of my tucking her in at night. She needed the protection of the nest to be assured that all was right with the world. She could assert her independence because she had a dependable place to come back to at the end of the day.

I think all people search for boundaries. It's the boundaries that make it possible to venture out and try new things, be independent, and explore new places and ideas. Boundaries give us security and a framework from which to grow, but in many ways our society has moved toward an elimination of boundaries. This is not a mature growth into freedom; it is a childish denial that boundaries are needed.

In our culture the denial of boundaries manifests itself in the form of relativism. When everything is judged from an individual perspective there are no absolutes. There are no clear boundaries. There is no clear right and wrong, no yardstick for decision making. Each person has his or her own set of rules or lack of rules. This form of relativism is the epitome of narcissism. It makes a god out of each individual.

Relativism is an imposter. It acts like freedom and tolerance but holds the promise of neither. It looks like freedom because it says everything is right or wrong depending on the individual point of view, but it leaves the mind in chaos, searching for some absolute starting point. The mind looks for things that in any circumstance must be wrong or right. Flying a plane into a building must be absolutely wrong, but there were people celebrating it as a victory over evil. To them it was Goliath receiving a mighty blow from David. True freedom originates from a place of security. We can criticize our government because we are secure that the system will not collapse under scrutiny. When my children were small they could lash out, saying, "I hate you Mommy," while knowing that I would love them anyway. The security comes from a familial and societal agreement that there are absolutes; for example, my right to protest by swinging my fist stops at the tip of your nose.

Relativism feels like tolerance; it makes the heart feel comfortable in its ability to accept others. But it is a lie. True tolerance comes from a secure place, where I know what I believe, and those beliefs are so secure that I don't need to find or force agreement in everyone else. Relativism comes from insecurity, where the heart has no clear vision or belief, so all beliefs must be an option, no matter how extreme.

People react to the culture of relativism in a number of ways. One way is to mimic the lack of boundaries of the culture. The person who reacts in this way must continually evaluate their worth, depending on ever-changing reference points. Relative judgment fluctuates, depending on the circumstances. I'm a success compared to one group but a failure based on the criteria of another. I'm a good mother if I stay home with my children. I'm a strong woman if I work outside the home. When the reference point fluctuates with time or with the situation there is no solid base from which to grow. When the reference point is actually many points there is no true identity. When there are many idols—like the idols of money, power, status, or beauty—there is no one absolute God. The heart and mind are left in chaos. Our society has been seduced by relativism, where boundaries shift, because they see no one orienting point of reference.

Another reaction to relativism is setting *external* boundaries and limits but having difficulty with *personal* boundaries. I count myself as one of those who finds it hard to set personal boundaries. I've worked hard these past few years to stop reflexively responding "yes" to every request. Even when my plate is full, I feel compelled to volunteer for the next committee or worthy cause. My husband, unfortunately, is no better than I am, so we overcommit ourselves without even realizing it. It is a constant struggle for us to set limits, especially on our time. We have had to realize that saying "yes" has a cost, and that cost is often high.

Joe Dominguez and Vicki Robin, in their book *Your Money or Your Life*, suggest that we put a monetary value on our time; each time we commit to something we should analyze how much it will "cost" us. Time is a commodity we can't produce more of, can't exchange or retrieve once it's spent. My husband and I can admit, looking back, that our choices were sometimes unwise. We didn't always realize the cost of not setting boundaries on our time. Our relationships with each other, our children, and our God have suffered because we did not guard our time. I now try to discern where I spend my time by determining my true motivations and the cost.

Another reaction to the cultural lack of boundaries caused by relativism is to set too many or too difficult boundaries. When people search for but cannot find boundaries, like those given to the Israelites or the babies in my unit, they seek any boundaries, even if they are harsh and unforgiving. If the soul is not oriented in God, it searches for other points of reference. The strict rules and regulations of any society or religion can bring security.

Fundamentalists look for comfort in law and order. They look for rigid and clear boundaries that define themselves and others as good or bad, saved or condemned. The intransigent viewpoint may appear to some as the antidote for the insecurity of our culture, but it is not. For some it may even be a place to start, but it is not the goal. Sooner or later those kinds of boundaries fall short because they do not allow us to grow.

The complexity of both life and people calls us to discernment with a formed consciousness, not just a blind obedience to the law. The law becomes the catalyst for looking further to where the law doesn't seem to fit. What about the person who kills in self-defense? Who can blame the starving man for coveting his neighbor's goods? What about the person who breaks the Sabbath by pulling his mule out of a ditch as it says in Matthew 12:11? In his letter to the Romans, Paul says that the function of the law is to show us that we can't rely on it; we must rely on a relationship with God. The law may be a place to start in order to give security to a society but it is only a means to an end. The law must lead us onward toward mercy, compassion, reconciliation, and relationship.

We should remember that Jesus was a Jew who grew up knowing the "law and the prophets." Luke says he grew in size, strength, and wisdom with the grace of God upon him (Lk 2:52). He grew in the customs of a Jewish home and community. Within the security of those traditions he grew into a mature relationship as the Son of God. Jesus had to show the people of his time that the law could not save them; it was only a place to start. He told them, "Do not think that I have come to abolish the law or the prophets; I have come not to abolish but to fulfill" (Mt 5:17). He said as much when he broke the Sabbath laws. He wasn't denying the importance of the Sabbath. He was showing them that keeping the Sabbath regulations was not the goal; it was the means to an end. The regulations brought the law to fulfillment by moving us toward a relationship with God. The soul seeks God, not the law. Jesus could say with authority and freedom that the Sabbath was made for man, not man for the Sabbath.

Having come from an obedient Jewish family, Jesus could see the function of the laws and regulations. He could also see that the law sometimes was elevated above the people whom God so dearly loved. Jesus told us that the law was given to us, not to replace God, but to help us grow into a mature relationship with God. John says of Jesus, "The law indeed was given through Moses; grace and truth came through Jesus Christ" (Jn 1:17). The law was given to us by Moses and it had to come first; then Jesus could lead us into the freedom of a relationship with God.

The law—the commandments such as "Keep holy the Sabbath"—is the nest we need to help us develop and grow when our relationship with God is not yet fully mature. We need to continually come back to Sabbath because the seduction of the culture is so strong. The Sabbath was commanded because it gives us a framework from which to grow. It keeps us looking onward toward a relationship with God. Sabbath reminds us that there is one absolute, one reference point, and one place to find our security. God gave us the Sabbath to reground our lives in him.

Sabbath and Sheves are related Hebrew words—Sheves means "to dwell." On the Sabbath God made the world his dwelling place in a special way. We can only be the dwelling place of God if we have a discipline to protect our time with God. A vessel is able to be filled because it has strong walls. The integrity of the vessel depends on the solid boundaries protecting that inner space. The Kabbalah teaches:

> Shabbot is much more than a day of rest. Rather it is a time of intense activity in the spiritual dimension, when the light of the Creator fills our hearts and minds to the greatest possible extent. We must prepare ourselves to be a fitting vessel that can contain the full abundance of the Creator's gift. For what good is the gift if there is no vessel capable of receiving it?

If I desire that God make his dwelling place in me, then I must make a protected holy time and place within my life to receive that gift. Celebrating Sabbath by excluding things of the world for some period of time, by saying no to yet another activity on a specific day, puts boundaries around that time and space and allows God to dwell in me. He commanded his people to form a nest around the Sabbath so that on that holy day they would remember that there is only one God and that they were children of God. Sabbath was instituted so there would not be an empty cycle of days but, as Bernard Anderson said in *Understanding the Old Testament,* "times embraced by God's purpose for Israel and all humankind." Jesus showed us that keeping the Sabbath holy is a necessary place to start so that we can grow and develop into a more mature relationship with God and with his people. When we do that we will be making the Sabbath, and every other day, holy.

FOR MEDITATION:

Look at a vessel. The only reason it functions is because the inner space is protected by the walls of the vessel. The vessel cannot be filled unless the boundaries are stable. The boundaries protect the inner space. What do the boundaries of your spiritual vessel look like?
- How am I grounded in a relationship with God?
- Do I protect my inner space?
- How am I a container for God's presence?

FOR DISCUSSION OR JOURNALING:

What are my boundaries?
What are the things I most believe in?
Do I protect those things?

If you are wise then you will show yourself a reservoir and not a canal. For a canal pours out as fast as it takes in; but a reservoir waits till it is full before it overflows, and so communicates its surplus.

—SAINT BERNARD OF CLAIRVAUX

5

The Gift of Covenant

Therefore the Israelites shall keep the sabbath, observing the sabbath throughout their generations, as a perpetual covenant. It is a sign forever between me and the people of Israel. . . .

— EXODUS 31:16–17

Sabbath is the sign of our everlasting covenant relationship with God. The primary gift of Sabbath is covenant and the primary function of Sabbath is the practice of our love relationship with God. Everything in life flows from and has meaning because of a loving relationship with God. God told his people through the prophets that the Sabbath would be the sign and symbol of their covenant. Sabbath is the sign and symbol of the relationship between God and mankind. God took his people as his bride and family. Unlike the marriage vows today, where more than half end in divorce, God's covenant is an everlasting bond. This relationship between God and his children is stronger than a contract, stronger than our promises, and as Paul teaches, even stronger than the bonds of blood. This covenant is to be an unbreakable love relationship where nothing is held back from the other.

When I look at scripture it seems that the relationship between God and his people starts unilaterally. God is the parent and the people are children. God doesn't appear to expect his people to be able to hold up their side of the covenant. The book of Deuteronomy is almost a litany of the times that Israel was unfaithful to God. He gives them Sabbath to remind them of his love and fidelity. He loves them through it all.

It is like the unconditional love of a parent. My mother used to say that she loved all ten of her children, "each one differently, but the same." I asked her how she could love each one of us that way. Mom said that each time she had a child it wasn't like another piece of the pie was taken. Instead, her ability to love grew exponentially. That is the generative nature of love. Then she said I wouldn't understand until I was a mother.

Of course, she was right. Becoming a parent gave me a completely different image of God and understanding of love. As each of my children grew inside me I fell in love with him or her—sight unseen, personality unknown, future unpredictable. It was complete and uncomplicated. It was relatively easy to love a baby even through hours of crying with some illness.

The teenage years have become the real growth period for us all. When my husband and I took our daughter to college I'm sure she was nervous and afraid. She expressed her fears through irritable, condescending, ungrateful behavior. By the end of "moving-in day" any rational person would be glad to leave, but all I could do was stand there and hold her, fighting my urge to pack her up and take her back home with me. Even when she was being awful to us, she was still my little girl. If she had broken the covenant of love with us in that moment, we would not have been able to break with her.

A covenant relationship requires a commitment and the discipline to carry it out. God made a covenant with the Israelites during a time in history when one nation could be conquered by another. The defeated were assimilated into the culture of the victors or they were eliminated. The defeated people lost their culture, their religion, their very identity; they took on the religion and culture of the conquerors. God chose the Israelites as an example of his lasting commitment. He gave them the Sabbath as a sign of his fidelity and as a way that they could learn fidelity. He would be their God regardless of whom they defeated or who defeated them. They could no longer be melded into another people, for they were God's people. The Israelites were scattered to the four winds, but they never lost their identity as the people of the covenant. Through the centuries God has remained faithful to his children. God became the example of commitment. It is said that "the Sabbath has kept Israel, more than Israel has kept the Sabbath." This is an honest admission that the celebration of Sabbath has served more as a reminder of God's fidelity to us than a practice of our fidelity to him.

We live in a time when most of us are shaped by the culture. It may be more subtle, but it is just as pervasive. Through peer pressure we learned very early how to conform to the culture, how to be politically correct. The values of my culture became my own before I was mature enough to examine those values. Sometimes I find it hard to distance myself from the culture, but God does not abandon me. He still claims me as his own, even if I do not always claim him. Even when I was not faithful to a practice of Sabbath he still upheld his side of the covenant.

In Jesus the covenant with God comes to full fruition. Jesus is symbolic of the new Israel: with him the covenant becomes mutual. In Jesus Israel is redeemed, and we see how to give and receive covenant love. He modeled this mutual indwelling throughout his life. Thomas Merton says that our relationship with God will grow no further than our most advanced human relationship. Maybe that's why most of us are called to the vocations of relationship: marriage, family, community life. We get to know the love of God through a selfless love of others which we experience by loving a spouse, child, friends. We learn that a sacrifice is not really a sacrifice; it's just what needs to happen in order to love someone. Forgiveness, compromise, and self-examination become part of the deal. We learn more about ourselves by looking through the eyes of another and may be inspired to adjust our personalities to be less offensive and more loving. Hopefully our ability to love will mature and grow.

The images we hold of our spouse and children change over time because we have more experiences with and knowledge of them. My image of God will change as I gain knowledge and experience of him through prayer, through others, and through the created world. Sabbath is an opportunity to increase our experience and knowledge of God to develop the kind of intimate relationship with the Father that Jesus showed us was possible.

The verse "I am the way, and the truth, and the life. No one comes to the Father except through me" (Jn 14:6) has always been problematic for me. That verse has been used to justify such violence in history, but I can't believe in a God who would create people if he didn't want to live in communion with them. Two-thirds of the world's population is non-Christian. My God could not be so limited as to only speak to a third of the world. Some non-Christians have followed the teachings of Jesus far better than I could ever hope to follow them.

Reading scripture in the context of the time is always helpful, but reading that verse in the context of covenant love clarifies it for me. Jesus is the revelation of the heart of God. He is a loving relationship with God. He always pointed beyond himself to God and to that relationship. Jesus is saying to me in that verse, "I'm showing you how to give and receive love from the Father. I'm inviting you into that covenant of love." The verse is certainly true; the only way to God is through a loving relationship with him. The Spirit also, in its many forms and many names, gives us access to that loving relationship. The way, the truth, and the life is through love. By practicing love we will know the God who is love.

Our God is a relational being. The Father, Son, and Holy Spirit exist in loving relationship. God so loved the world that he sent his only Son. It was love that moved Jesus to open his arms on the cross to each of us. Jesus described, and, more important, he lived the covenant relationship. Then he went further and invited each of us to join in that loving relationship, when he said in so many ways what was recorded in John 17:21: "As you, Father, are in me and I am in you, may they also be in us, so that the world may believe that you have sent me." When Jesus left, he gave us the Spirit, so that wherever two or three were gathered he would be there. The Father's love generates the Son and the Spirit proceeds from that love. It took us a few hundred years after the death of Jesus to put all this into words.

We call that loving relationship between Father, Son, and Spirit the Trinity. The Trinity is a loving symbiosis. Generative love is the basis of our understanding of the Trinity. The very nature of God is relational and communal, and God made us in that image and likeness. We were made to be in relationship through him and in him. Saint Augustine said, "You have made us for yourself and our hearts are restless until they rest in you." Julian of Norwich, a mystic, also spoke of our need to be in relationship with God, saying, "For by our nature our will wants God and the good will of God wants us."

This I know for sure, that God has invited me into the loving relationship that is the Trinity. I may live in this world, a world of producing, achieving, and building walls and masks, but my soul belongs to another world. My soul knows a deeper truth, a deeper reality. If I want to be in relationship with God then I need to come to the party, but I can't dance with God if I'm busy dancing with the idols of this world. God invited me to break periodically from this world and come to his party. The invitation he offered is Sabbath. I get lots of junk mail, so I'm sure there have been times that I've missed his invitation amidst the junk. I think for a long time I missed Sabbath. But God continued to pursue me and he sent another invitation, a more profound one this time. In Jesus I am taught not only how to recognize the invitation into the relationship of the Trinity but also how to receive it, accept it, and respond to it.

Jesus was able to have Sabbath moments whenever he chose because he was fully a part of the relationship. I must start small with more defined times to concentrate on what it means and how it feels to be in that Trinity relationship. I have to look for God somewhere before I can recognize him everywhere. In Jesus, who is one with the Father and lives on in the Spirit, the covenant bond is completed and exemplified. Jesus shows us the way and becomes the way we accept God's invitation to join in the covenant love of the Trinity.

We build the covenant relationship through the practice of Sabbath. God said that keeping the Sabbath would be symbolic of our covenant relationship with him. A symbol is most effective when it closely depicts the real life action that it represents; therefore, the practice of Sabbath should be a practice in relationship. Sabbath is our opportunity to spend time with God. The specific day is not as important as the consistent time I put aside to invest in an intimate relationship with God. I try to practice Sabbath so that I recognize and nurture a relationship. Practicing Sabbath is a conscious effort to make a space for the ultimate relationship.

When my husband and I went on a Marriage Encounter we were taught how to communicate better with each other. They encouraged us to "dialogue" with each other for at least twenty minutes a day. This dialogue had to be of a specific type. It couldn't be about who was taking the kids to the dentist or who would stop at the store. We learned to write letters to each other about our feelings, aspirations, and concerns. Then we exchanged the letters and discussed them. The conversations took us to a deeper level. To me, dialoguing sounds a lot like a practice of daily prayer.

The other major recommendation to help us keep our marriage on track was that we have a weekly date night. Counselors and marriage improvement programs often recommend a date night for couples. It is a time each week when we set aside work and the world so that we can focus on our relationship and on each other. My husband and I know that date night is a good, vital practice. Too often we get busy and put each other on the back burner, but before long one of us will point out that we need to reconnect. Then we recommit ourselves to the practice of dialogue and date night. Any relationship requires time and energy. A relationship with God is no different. Sabbath is like having a date night with God.

In order to move toward a mature, mutual relationship with God, we have to make the relationship a priority. We must be committed. Eric Liddell is a modern Christian example of that commitment. He was Scotland's best hope for a gold medal in the 1924 Paris Olympics. His story was told in the movie *Chariots of Fire*. Liddell refused to run his best event, the 100-meter sprint, because it was held on the Lord's Day (his Sabbath). Initially, he was condemned by the Scottish press. After all, he had been sent to represent a people whose sense of nationalism should take priority over his personal values. He could celebrate the Sabbath the next day. Certainly God would understand. You might expect that his coach, of all people, would try to convince him to run. But instead Liddell was inspired to keep his commitment by a note from his coach that said, "He who honors him, he [God] will honor." Liddell kept his commitment to God. He did not run his best event; instead, Liddell ran and won the gold medal in the 400-meter race the next day.

My commitment to honoring time with God is much less dramatic, but even my flimsy efforts at keeping Sabbath have helped me understand how necessary that commitment is. I have moments of Sabbath with a practice of daily prayer and an effort to discern God's will in the choices I make. Prayer helps me become attuned to God's manifestations in the world and in my life. It is my effort to listen to God. I make choices a hundred times a day that are either for or against love, whether I recognize them or not. A daily commitment to prayer helps me to recognize and better make those choices. I have to schedule a time for prayer or it ends up being the last thing on my "to do" list, the thing that never gets done.

The same is true for Sabbath. I recognize that I need an extended period of time to express my commitment to God and to build a relationship with him. I have no doubt that a commitment to God will require sacrifices, just as a commitment to my husband and children have required sacrifices through the years. My husband and I realized during the Marriage Encounter that our marriage wouldn't just take care of itself. We had to make it a priority, but we couldn't just say it. We had to back it up in practice everyday. We had to start setting some time aside just for us.

Practicing Sabbath means that I have to reserve that day on my calendar to mark it as a priority, and then schedule my other activities around it. Each week I need to get away from the activities of work, running errands, or completing projects to have a date with God. I need that time to develop my commitment to a relationship with God and to receive again his love and commitment to me.

Nothing is more important than the relationship between two people. When they realize they are connected they become closer to God.

—MARTIN BUBER

FOR MEDITATION:

Make a list of the most important things in your life. Look at your calendar for the last few weeks and list the activities that occupied your time. Does your time spent reflect your priorities? What does your calendar say about your priorities?

- Do I spend some quality time with God each day? Why or why not?

- When I look at the things that occupy my money and time, what do they say about my values?
- How do my human relationships reflect my relationship with God?

FOR DISCUSSION OR JOURNALING:

If I imagined a perfect relationship with God, what would it be like?

FOR THE WEEK AHEAD:

Set twenty minutes aside each day for silent prayer.

They entered into a covenant to seek the LORD, the God of their ancestors, with all their heart and with all their soul. . . . All Judah rejoiced over the oath; for they had sworn with all their heart, and had sought him with their whole desire, and he was found by them, and the LORD gave them rest all around.

—2 CHRONICLES 15:12, 15

6

The Gift of New Creation

> So if anyone is in Christ, there is a new creation: everything old has passed away; see, everything has become new!

> —2 CORINTHIANS 5:17

Friday evening to Saturday evening is the seventh day, the Sabbath for Orthodox Jews, their most sacred day of the week. The first followers of Christ, many of whom were Jews, continued to celebrate the Sabbath. Then on Sunday, early in the morning before going off to work, they also celebrated a special meal, which was later called the eucharist. The Sabbath was supplanted by Sunday as the most holy day of the week for Christians for two reasons. First, the Jewish followers of Christ became estranged from their Jewish communities and were eventually expelled from the Jewish temple. The split was often a bitter one and so led to the Christian's rejection or substitution of Jewish tradition for new Christian practices. Second, the ranks of Christians were increasingly made up of gentiles, who did not come from a tradition of practicing the Sabbath. The eucharistic meal became the central symbol and action of the Christian communities.

Centuries later, with the dawn of the five-day workweek Sunday took on the flavor of the Sabbath. The weekend was the time of rest before going back to start work on the first day of the "workweek." Most Christians to this day think of Sunday as our holy day of the week.

Sunday was the pagan word for what the Jews called the first day of the week, but Christians had many names for their special day of worship. They called it "little Easter," "the day of resurrection," or the day of "new birth" to commemorate the resurrection of Jesus. It was a day to celebrate the rebirth of Jesus and all of us with him. They also called it the "eighth" day to make it known that this was a new day in a new age of Christ, not the first day of just another week. All the names commemorated new life. The "eighth day," in particular, signified the fullness of a new creation. They were celebrating the dawn of a new world where God would reign. They celebrated Christ's rising to new life and bringing us into that new life with him. I love the Jewish concept of the Sabbath rest and I have merged it with my Christian belief in new creation. Having Sabbath on Sunday, the eighth day of the week, reminds me that God is the eternal creator.

When I am going through difficult times I look forward to the end of the emotional and sometimes physical stress and fatigue, but I also look for the light at the end of the tunnel, when "normal" life might begin again. Years ago, when I was in a place of spiritual and emotional darkness, I couldn't see even a glimmer of light ahead; in fact, there seemed to be no end in sight. My first instinct was to try to solve my way out of the darkness. When that didn't work I fell back into my usual pattern, which was to try harder to solve my way out.

The problem was not something that I could control or solve. Finally I had to just be in that dark and lonely place. God didn't change my situation, but he was there with me in the darkness so I was not alone. The resolution was not a quick fix; it took time and it involved much turmoil. The result was not what I expected or even imagined.

One of the outcomes was a new image of God. I already saw God as a father figure, a friend and counselor, but now he was also the creator. It may seem strange that God as creator was a new image, but it was an image I only knew abstractly from Genesis and science. I never really thought of God as the ongoing creator. I hadn't thought of him as a personal creator with immeasurable imagination. The scripture "For my thoughts are not your thoughts, nor are your ways my ways, says the LORD" (Is 55:8) had new meaning. I should not depend on or be led to despair by my limited ability to comprehend or solve problems. Instead I should depend on the perpetually creative nature of God. That new image of God became important years later when I was talking to a friend one Sunday afternoon.

My husband and I had been in a couples prayer group for ten years with three other couples. A member of the group called one Sunday. Steve was in crisis. He had been suffering for more than a year after having back surgery that didn't seem to be healing. Upon further evaluation he was diagnosed with Parkinson's disease. He was in declining health, which seemed to intensify the marital difficulties he and his wife had been having for years. She had just recently left with their two teenage daughters. His daughters no longer wanted him to be a part of their lives. He was alone and severely depressed when he called.

As he talked I became concerned that he might be suicidal and so I asked him if he had ever thought about it. He said "yes." He felt it might be the best thing for him and his family. No one would have to take care of him as his condition declined and he would not have to endure any more physical or emotional pain. It all seemed to make sense to him. He felt that God must be "calling him home" because he couldn't think of any other ending to this story. I asked him if he thought that God might be able to create a new ending, one that Steve hadn't thought of yet. I asked him to wonder with me about all the possibilities that we could imagine. What if in a year or two one of his daughters was in crisis and realized she still needed and loved her father? He would need to be here for that possibility. We talked through a few more scenarios. In the end he had to admit that neither one of us could fully imagine what God might eventually create in his life. Committing suicide would be like saying that his powers to solve the problem were greater than God's creativity.

About six months after our conversation, Steve's oldest daughter, Jessie, became pregnant. She felt alone and unsupported by the father of the baby. Jessie's mother was busy with a new relationship of her own, so she asked Jessie to leave. She had nowhere to go. Jessie needed her dad. She moved back home and they went through the pregnancy and the first year of his grandchild's life together. Steve's face lights up whenever he is around his baby granddaughter. His other daughter moved back home and they all support and take care of each other. He tells me they are a closer family now than he ever could have imagined.

The past was very painful but the new relationships and insights were outcomes Steve never anticipated. He still mourns the loss of his marriage and the future he dreamed of but he is grateful for the new life he has now. What I didn't find out until recently was that during our Sunday conversation, Steve had been sitting with a gun in his lap.

So often in scripture we are asked to look beyond ourselves to God's creative power. Mary and Zechariah had differing responses to the angel of God, because one had difficulty believing in the creative nature of God and the other did not. Zechariah, the priest married to Elizabeth, was told by the angel that Elizabeth would bear a son. Zechariah and Elizabeth were both old and Elizabeth had always been sterile. Although Zechariah may have welcomed a blessing from God, this one was too much for him to imagine. This blessing was too unexpected, too impossible. He doubted, asking the angel for proof (Lk 1:18). Instead he was struck mute until after the birth of his son. At the naming ritual he finally regained his voice to do what the angel commanded by naming the child John. Zechariah did not believe in the eternally creative nature of God so he was left unable to speak of it.

Mary, on the other hand, had a few logistical questions for the angel Gabriel but never doubted God. Even though she did not feel worthy of this gift, even though she did not understand it, she welcomed God's creation with open arms. Some might see the months when Zechariah was mute as a punishment for doubting God. But maybe it was another blessing. Maybe Zechariah used his time in silence to learn how to listen more attentively to God. Maybe it was a time when he, too, needed to develop and be reborn.

Zechariah and Mary were asked to see a world beyond their own reasoning or imagination. Jesus broke the apostles out of their standard way of thinking. In the gospel of Mark, Jesus shared with the disciples that he expected to suffer and die.

> Then he began to teach them that the Son of Man must undergo great suffering, and be rejected by the elders, the chief priests, and the scribes, and be killed, and after three days rise again. He said all this quite openly. And Peter took him aside and began to rebuke him. But turning and looking at his disciples, he rebuked Peter and said, "Get behind me, Satan! For you are setting your mind not on divine things but on human things" (Mk 8:31–33).

Peter was reflectively reacting to the terrifying news with a fight or flight response. Jesus' words were intended to shake Peter out of his trance, allowing him to see an alternative. Peter had not even considered that God could have been creating another way.

Most of what Jesus tells us requires that we trust in the creative nature of God. He tells us of a God who is present and merciful, whose name is "Abba," and of a kingdom that promises true freedom and justice, but with peace. The sons of Zebedee liked the idea of a new kingdom, but they were still in their trance. So they sent their mother to acquire places of honor for them. She asked Jesus to command that in the new kingdom her sons would sit at his right and left hand (Mt 20:21). They fit the kingdom of God into their idea of what a kingdom was like on earth. They didn't hear that this was a new kind of kingdom, where kings were servants to all and the first would be last.

Jesus often used parables to break the disciples out of their cultural trance, and the parables still have that effect on us today if we let them. Parables were meant to lead us down the typical path. But just when we thought we knew who was good and who was bad and how things would neatly come out in the end, the story would flip and everything would turn upside down. The unexpected ending makes us reconsider our assumptions and expectations. In Matthew 13:13 Jesus said, "The reason I speak to them in parables is that 'seeing they do not perceive, and hearing they do not listen, nor do they understand.'" He was speaking about people in a trance. They, like us, were living in a place where they subconsciously followed the rules and messages of the culture.

The messages—like materialism, individualism, or nationalism—are so imbedded that we don't even consider anything else. In fact, we live by the assumptions without thinking about them at all, unless an event breaks us from our trance. We assume that if we work hard we will succeed, until we have a child who can't seem to learn how to control his behavior no matter how hard he tries, or until we are the one who is laid off yet again. We want to believe that the only way to stop a bully is to hit harder and with a bigger bat; no other response is worth considering.

I listen to the news about so many places in the world where people have been fighting and killing each other for thousands of years. It seems like it will never end. But I wonder if it continues because we all live in our trances, without hope of a different outcome. We want quick answers that will be lasting, but our repertoire of solutions seems very limited. Like Peter, we react without considering that there may be something different than we expect at the end of the road. What if we dared to imagine or, even more than that, dared to have faith in something beyond our imagination?

Then we might be open to the creative nature of God. Then there might be hope for peace, freedom, justice, and life.

I don't believe that I am a pawn on God's chessboard. I don't believe that each day he makes a specific plan for me. I believe that if I live with the simple intent of nurturing an intimate relationship with God and with his creation, then I will be following his will, his plan for me. But that can take me down many roads. Some roads will be difficult and painful while other roads will be wonderful. The difficult times may have been caused by my poor choices or by the poor choices of others. If I make loving choices, it does not mean I will have a life without pain; in fact it probably promises the opposite. The mystic Julian of Norwich said, "First there is the fall and then there is the recovery from the fall. But both are the mercy of God." He travels a path with me that is ever-changing and ever-new because I am ever-changing. It's my experience that life is messy, but, regardless of the situation, God perpetually assures me, saying, "I can work with this too."

So if anyone is in Christ, there is a new creation: everything old has passed away; see, everything has become new!

—2 CORINTHIANS 5:17

FOR MEDITATION:

Take a walk and observe the wonders of nature, from the ants working on their anthill to the mighty oak. Meditate about a God who cares so much for all he has created. Think about the seasons and the cycle of many deaths and rebirths that we all experience.

- What things or people do I turn to in times of stress?
- Where do I find hope?
- How do I react to unexpected turns in life?
- Do I only seek out God for a solution in troubled times?
- Are there times when I have trusted my own solutions over God's?
- Does God's timeline fit my own?
- When has my blindness/trance been broken by God's creative love for me?
- How can I be a gift of creation for others?

FOR DISCUSSION OR JOURNALING:

Share a time when you were surprised by an unexpected turn of events or outcome.

C reation draws us into the very life
of the creator.

—CONSTITUTION ON THE
SACRED LITURGY

7

The Gift of Presence

> . . . I am with you always, to the end of
> the age.
>
> —MATTHEW 28:20

Sabbath is about being present in the moment. It's about God's presence. We can only experience God in the present moment. We can't experience him in the past or the future. Sequential time is our limitation, not his. We live in *chronos*—the Greek word for linear time. But there is another word for time—*kairos*. It is the word for God's time or holy time. It cannot be measured in minutes or hours; its effects are for all time. I've heard *kairos* described as "God's time of grace." It is the time and space where we can meet God. Our faith is not possible except that God became present and wants to be present in relationship with us. But how is he present and how can we respond to his presence?

In scripture, God is present in many forms. During the Exodus he was present to Moses. When Moses asked who would accompany him on the journey, God promised Moses that "my presence will go with you, and I will give you rest" (Ex 33:14). God was present to Samuel as a voice in a dream. Mary and others felt the presence of God through a messenger.

Jesus brought us a little closer to the presence of God. Jesus told us about an intimate relationship with the father. He told us of a God who is always in our midst. He told us of a father who has counted the hairs on our heads and knows our needs better than we know ourselves. Jesus became the presence of God by being present to those around him, especially to those in need. Through Jesus we can see and touch the heart of God, we can experience him face to face. Through Jesus, God enters *chronos* and transforms it into *kairos*. Consider the story of the woman he healed:

> Now there was a woman who had been suffering from hemorrhages for twelve years. She had endured much under many physicians, and had spent all that she had; and she was no better, but rather grew worse. She

had heard about Jesus, and came up behind him in the crowd and touched his cloak, for she said, "If I but touch his clothes, I will be made well." Immediately her hemorrhage stopped; and she felt in her body that she was healed of her disease. Immediately aware that power had gone forth from him, Jesus turned about in the crowd and said, "Who touched my clothes?" And his disciples said to him, "You see the crowd pressing in on you; how can you say, 'Who touched me?'" He looked all around to see who had done it. But the woman, knowing what had happened to her, came in fear and trembling, fell down before him, and told him the whole truth. He said to her, "Daughter, your faith has made you well; go in peace, and be healed of your disease" (Mk 5:25–34).

Although there was a lot of activity, and Jesus was surrounded by people, he was still fully conscious of this moment. He was so aware that he could sense the woman touching his cloak, or he may have felt her need. He stopped what he was doing and attended to her. At that moment she must have felt that the world had stopped. Her fear turned to wonder and gratitude as he looked into her eyes. The world was caught between them in that moment. As I read that story, I wondered what it might be like to look into the eyes of Jesus and have the world stand still. What must it have been like for the present and eternity to become one?

Reflecting on this passage one day I realized that I had seen that look before. Moments like that exist when parents look at their infant in the Neonatal Intensive Care Unit. The infant looks up to the parent and the parent down on the child and they are caught in each other's gaze. They are lost

in each other. I remember looking at my babies the same way.
I could have looked at them for hours, not noticing the time.
The world is contained in that moment. There is no rush to
the next moment, no worry about the past, there is only now.
That night I wrote my reflection in my prayer journal:

> Do you look upon me that way, Lord? Teach
> me how to return your gaze. I feel unworthy,
> I tend to drop my eyes, but are you calling me
> to look back?

> *I am calling you, always. Don't let the moment
> pass in your anxiety, guilt, or fear. Look to me
> and press on. I will hold you in my gaze.*

> I'm afraid that if I look upon you I will be lost
> and not able to look away.

> *I will tell you, you will be lost, but lost in your
> deepest self. Looking to me does not take you
> away from yourself, it brings you closer. When
> you look upon me you see the truest you and the
> whole of humanity as well. You will see what can
> be, you will see hope.*

> If I look to you, it's only for a moment. It
> passes too quickly. I retreat from you again.
> How do I learn to live in that moment?

> *Just take the first step. I show you how, when you
> look at your infants and when you see others do
> the same. Walk as if you have faith and you will
> have it. Retreating from me is merely another
> opportunity to come home to me. Look at your
> children and see them look at you. Really see them
> for who they are. Love them for who I made them
> to be. Allow them to love you. Share the gaze with
> them—it will teach you both.*

We all have moments when the spirit breaks through. The question is, do we recognize those moments of grace? How many times have I missed the miracle because I'm just not paying attention? Children are naturals at this kind of living in and attending to God's presence and I believe they can teach us. Years ago when my children were toddlers, I was going back and forth between making dinner, doing laundry, and sewing a pair of pants for the kids while the two of them were running around an obstacle course in the playroom. As I stood by the stove, trying to figure out what to do next so I could be efficient with my time, both of them came in and pulled on my leg. I bent down to see what they needed. First one then the other put their little hands on my cheeks just like I always did with them, kissed me, and said, "Love you, Mommy." At that moment my world stopped, because the real world broke through. God's grace was in that moment.

There are other times when I suddenly become aware of God's presence. When I see a sunset over the ocean I'm awash with a feeling of gratitude and awe. Suddenly the sound of someone laughing becomes contagious. My day is given new perspective because my child reaches up to hold my hand. A piece of music inexplicably brings me to tears. We all have had moments when our linear time is made holy by God's grace. These are times when we let go of ourselves, our ego consciousness, and for that moment we transcend and meet God. Most of the time I'm surprised by these moments when God catches me off guard, but I think we can also develop a sensitivity for the transcendent, like the trained eye of the sculptor who learns to see the finished form in a block of clay. I think we can develop a way of being in the moment.

Rabbi Lawrence Kushner suggests in his book *Jewish Spirituality* that there was a reason God presented himself to Moses as a burning bush. God could have come in the form of something grand and spectacular. Instead, he used the modest miracle of a burning bush. Kushner explains that "Moses had to stop and watch the flames long enough to realize that the branches were not being consumed." Moses had to pay attention to that seemingly ordinary thing in that ordinary moment; then God could speak to him.

One of the essential practices of Buddhism is to become mindful or awake. It means to be acutely aware of the present moment. The name Buddha means "the awakened one." Jesus was so attentive, so aware in the moment, that he could feel the woman who merely touched his cloak. Jesus was ready for the divine encounter in that moment and in every moment.

There are people who are gifted or who have cultivated a talent for being fully present in every moment. These people seem to live in *kairos*. I knew a man who had such a gift. He made connections with everyone he met. He died too young from complications of cancer. The resurrection Mass was filled with people who knew and loved John. One friend, feeling the pain of John's death, felt bitter that so many people were at his funeral invading his private time of mourning. But so many attended the Mass that day because John had been fully present to so many.

As people remembered him, there was a common thread in what they all saw in John and what I experienced when I was with him. They all said that no matter the situation John made them feel like they were the most important thing at that moment. He was fully present to them in that moment. He listened and responded with all of himself. He remembered small things about each person: the names of their children, where they grew up or where they had worked. He was generous in his affirmation and with his affection. Even during a brief encounter, John made each person feel special, and that connected them forever. Most people spoke of it as a talent or a gift *from* God, but I think what John really had was the gift *of* God. It was the gift of God's presence through John. He made people feel what Jesus promised when he said, "For where two or three are gathered in my name, I am there among them" (Mt 18:20).

My instinct is to say that John was just special; not everyone can be as he was. But this gift of presence is different from other gifts of the spirit, like preaching or healing. Those gifts are given to a specific few; the gift of God's presence is given to us all. What John showed me was how to use the gift of God's presence to the fullest. At his funeral I committed myself to learn from him and to model him—to be God's presence to others.

There is a legend that says that Saint Francis of Assisi was hoeing his garden one day when he was approached by one of the young friars. The young student asked Francis what he would be doing if he knew this was his last day to live. Francis replied, "I'd hoe my garden." Francis could say that because he lived every moment to the fullest. Why would he do something else when that moment, hoeing his garden, contained the fullness of life for him?

I have to wonder what my answer to that question would be. What would I do if I knew my time was limited? I'm sure that I would talk with my children and husband, family and friends. I'd laugh and cry with them. I'd hug and kiss them a lot. I'd tell them how special they are to me. I'd forgive what needs to be forgiven, and I'd ask for forgiveness and make amends if needed. I probably wouldn't do 90 percent of what I do each day of my life. What freedom Saint Francis showed to be able to say he would keep hoeing his garden!

To develop an eye of faith and the ability to live fully in the moment I first need to slow down. Father William McNamara wrote in his book *The Human Adventure*, "We will have to stop doing half the things we do in order to do the other half with faith and love." I can't possibly be conscious and aware of each moment in my day. Some days are so busy that I don't think I can be present in any moment. I can't even remember what I had for breakfast because I'm already planning what's for dinner. I can't be reflective when I'm just trying to keep my head above water. I can't be present for people if my mind is going a mile a minute or emotionally I'm tied up somewhere else.

I need time to practice gazing at the Lord by looking around me into the eyes of the people and things he loves. I need time to practice recognizing moments of grace. I need time to practice being in God's presence and being God's presence for others. One day I may be able to live fully conscious of God's grace while still doing my job and caring for my family, but until then I need to set aside time to practice being present in the moment. I need practice forming an intimate relationship with God so that he can be present to others through me. Sabbath is that time. Sabbath is a time when I consciously stop and live fully in each moment, when I live like Saint Francis.

Henri Nouwen told a story about a professor at the University of Notre Dame, who, reflecting on his life, said, "I have always been complaining that my work was constantly interrupted, until I slowly realized that my interruptions were my work." Sabbath interrupts our endless cycle of work and gives us the time to slow down, to reflect, and to gaze into the eyes of God. Sabbath is a time to be in God's presence and to be God's presence in the world. Sabbath time is *kairos*, the holy time of God's grace.

You cannot truly listen to anyone and do anything else at the same time.

—Scott Peck

FOR MEDITATION:

Reflect on your day. When today have you felt God's presence?

- Do you tend to live in the past, present, or future?
- Looking back over the last week, can you recognize moments of grace?
- Identify a few ways to be more present to the people you encounter.

FOR DISCUSSION OR JOURNALING:

Describe a time when you felt God's presence or when you were aware of being God's presence to someone else.

FOR THE WEEK AHEAD:

Write your own morning or evening prayer. Ask God to help you become more aware of his presence in your life. Recite that prayer each day for a week.

"Know that I am with you and will keep you wherever you go, and will bring you back to this land; for I will not leave you until I have done what I have promised you."

Then Jacob woke from his sleep and said, "Surely the LORD is in this place—and I did not know it!"

—GENESIS 28:15–16

8

The Gift of the Journey

He has told you, O mortal, what is good; and what does the LORD require of you but to do justice, and to love kindness, and to walk humbly with your God?

—MICAH 6:8

Sabbath was given as a way to journey with God. It gave the people of Israel a weekly discipline of remembering, listening, and recommitting themselves to a relationship with God. It became a tradition passed from one generation to the next. Sabbath reminded them to stop doing and pause for a moment to be with God. The Sabbath was like a stepping stone or reference point. People would refer to close friends by saying they had shared many Sabbaths. We share our lives with God when we share many Sabbaths with him.

The Bible is a history of the relationship between God and his creation, especially with those he made in his image. In the scriptures we read about the ups and downs of that relationship. In the Hebrew scriptures, the prophets remind people to stay in relationship with God by keeping the Sabbath. When people ignore God, they soon find that their world falls apart. The scriptures are replete with stories of God's faithfulness on this journey. He is a steadfast companion, no matter the circumstances. In fact, the circumstances become secondary to the realization that God is the ever-present companion. The object of the journey is to show people that God is present in all things and at all times.

I was told the Exodus story when I was a child and I remember it like a Charlton Heston movie. I remember thinking how strange it was that it took forty years to find the Promised Land, a trip that could have been made in a matter of weeks. But the people were not merely on a journey in the geographic sense. They were on a spiritual journey, the kind of journey that we all must take if we are to grow in relationship with God and with each other.

The enslaved people of Egypt were not one nationality; they were from many different lands, with differing beliefs and customs. Many of them did not believe in one god, let alone a God who wanted to be in relationship with them. It took this loosely gathered group years of traveling together to develop a relationship with each other and with God, until their very identity became united, a people of the one true God. It took more than a generation to develop the rituals, customs, practices, and traditions that bound them together and gave them their common identity.

So they journeyed forty years in the desert, often wanting to turn back or break from the group. They complained about the rules and practices, which sometimes seemed silly and useless but, in fact, it was those practices and that time frame that bound them together. Through it all, the people were changing and maturing in their relationship with God and each other. It was the journey, not the Promised Land, that made them a people of God.

The journey could not have been a straight path. The relationship needed to be built with time and experience, joy and tears, anger and forgiveness. That common identity forged in the desert still binds them together and to God after all these centuries. Even though modern-day Israelites are physically scattered to the wind, they are spiritually a people of God.

In the Christian scriptures, Jesus showed us the way into a deeper relationship with God. Jesus' missionary journey started after his baptism by John, when he went into the desert to meet God and face the temptations of humanity. Afterward, he gathered the disciples and shared the journey with them. The disciples and Jesus had time to establish deep commitments and trust. They traveled, worked, slept, ate, and prayed together. They shared many Sabbaths with each other. Jesus not only shared his thoughts and wisdom with them, but he also shared his life with them.

I've often wondered why Jesus didn't teach during the time between the resurrection and his ascension. He had been to the other side of death and could have given us so much information. Instead, there is a notable lack of teaching during this time: no parables, no lessons, no convincing arguments for the doubters. The disciples did not learn from the risen Jesus how to set up the church, who to welcome into their number, or what rituals to develop. There was so much more to know, but maybe they didn't need to *know* more. They needed Jesus' reassuring presence to remind them of what they had already experienced. The disciples had spent years with Jesus, and they needed to be assured that the relationship would continue. After Jesus' death the disciples were scattered, scared, unsure, and lost without direction, much as the Israelites had been time and again throughout history. Just as God had reminded the Israelites that they were not alone, so Jesus showed the disciples that their relationship continues and grows deeper still. That same journey continues with us today.

I grew up a little like those early Israelites—always moving around. My father's job took us from state to state. I learned to protect myself from getting too attached to any one place or people. The last time we moved it was my third high school in as many years. My parents brought me into their room last, after all my brothers and sisters, to break the news. As they told me, the room began to spin and I thought, "I'm just too tired." They later told me that I said those very words and then passed out cold. Everything in my life seemed transient. My only attachment was to my immediate family.

When I was in college, Sundays were my lonely days. The rest of the week was jam-packed with work, studying, meetings, or socializing, but on Sundays everything slowed down. I had a chance to wonder what was happening at home or with my brothers and sisters across the country. It made me sad that we were all so far apart, but phoning home brought me closer to them. Mom told me the news about everyone and I felt a little better.

Going to church also made me feel closer to them, because it was something we always did on Sunday. I was raised with God and the Catholic Church both very present in my life. Most of our family traditions revolved around religious holidays or Church practices, a reality with both a positive and negative side. On the positive side, those traditions kept me tied to my family and the Church, even when I traveled physically and mentally far away from them. On the other side, it probably led me to equate my image of God with my image of the Church. Therefore, when I felt rejected by the Church I felt rejected by God.

It took me some time and a lot of searching before I found my way back to the Church. That process was made possible by a healthy separation of my understanding of who God is versus my understanding of the Church. Now I am comfortable with an image of God that continues to change and grow as I continue to change and grow.

As I reflect on the years when I questioned the mere existence of God and searched for faith, I see that he was on that quest with me. I argued with God and searched for God, unable to hear his voice, but even when I felt very distant from God, I now see that he was present. My limitations didn't allow me to sense him. Even during the years when I was not present to God he was present to me. And our journey together continues.

There are opportunities to know God in all phases of the journey. We can know God during the spiritual peaks and know him in a different way when we are in the spiritual dark valleys or deserts. Most of my life has been on level terrain; that path, too, provides an opportunity to journey with God. But I have also had long periods of time in the desert when my prayer life seemed dry and God seemed very distant. Those times motivated me to pray. When life was difficult, I searched for meaning in events and people. The dark valleys brought insight into my darkness, and there I found hidden strengths. The difficult times made me change focus, letting go of my masks and the roles that I play. I had less need for approval because when my world was falling apart I had no energy to be concerned about the approval of others. Ironically, that brought a kind of freedom; I let go of my false security to find true security in God.

When my journey took me to a spiritual peak, I was moved to deep gratitude and an expanded image of God. I remember coming home to my dormitory after a retreat called "Encounter with Christ." I had experienced a very powerful weekend where I felt the love of God, probably for the first time. I returned to find my suitemates planning their next happy hour. They asked for my opinion on the theme. I burst out with, "What does it matter? There is a God!" My friends were confused and afraid I had become a "Jesus freak." In an effort to control my newfound enthusiasm, I tried to not speak to them until I could come down from that spiritual mountaintop. The experience made a connection between my head and my heart. I felt favored and chosen by God.

There are also opportunities on the flat lands, the level terrain, to feel a steady state of peace in the presence of God. The flat times can also require diligence, because relationships can slip away due to inattention. The plateaus in my journey have been times when I've had more energy because I was not encumbered or overwhelmed with emotional highs or lows. Therefore, I paid attention to detail. I used those times to look for God's presence in the ordinary things of life and in the small, seemingly insignificant encounters. I watched for indications of God's will and practiced discernment in small decisions, so I would be better prepared when the larger challenges came along.

Sabbath welcomes us and keeps us on the journey with God. Scripture reminds the people of God to let go of all the doing, all the distractions, so they can be with their traveling companion in a deeper way. In *Sabbatical Journey: The Diary of His Final Year*, Henri Nouwen said that the mission of his sabbatical was to deepen relationships with God and with others. He knew that he would have to let go of the things that made him feel significant and his addiction to being busy. Sabbath is a time of letting go of self-serving distractions so we can move to a deeper relationship with God.

The beauty of Sabbath is that it meets us wherever we are on the journey. All roads lead to God if we follow them—just keep on the road. Sabbath can be practiced in a myriad of ways. Initially, just following the rules and regulations can have some positive effects. Obedience to God's command, a discipline of trying to meet God each week, shows a profound commitment and openness to God. The act of stepping back and doing something countercultural offers a new perspective on life. Rest and relaxation can be revitalizing, at least momentarily. Hopefully, though, we will be led into deeper experiences with God through worship, fellowship, and prayer.

Sabbath is a time to look back at the journey. Sabbath is like the poem "Footprints," which tells of a man who looks back at the journey of his life and sees two sets of footprints in the sand. One set belongs to him and the other to God. During difficult times he sees only one set of footprints. The man asks God why, at the worst times, he was forced to walk the journey alone. God reassures the man that those were not times when he was alone; rather, during the hard times, God carried him.

Life is a journey of my own making. I can choose to walk with God or be blind to his presence, but even the times when I have been blind to his presence can be salvaged. No time is wasted because I can reflect on the important events, people, places, and experiences of my life. In hindsight I can see that God has always been with me on the journey. The Sabbath is a time to look back and see God's footprints in my life. It is a time to remember and be grateful for an ever-present God and to look forward to the Sabbaths still to come on the journey ahead.

O n the long journey of life, faith is the best of companions; it is the best refreshment on the journey and it is the greatest property.

—BUDDHA

FOR MEDITATION:

List the stepping stones of your life—the pivotal events and milestones. Also think of intense experiences; people who had an influence; and places, books, and music that carry meaning. Write them down as they come to you, not necessarily in any specific order. Reflect on the presence of God in those people, events, places or things. Make note of your feelings as you remember them.

- What are my first memories of God and prayer?
- What was my image of God during different stages of my life? (e.g., child, teen, young adult, etc.)
- Who have been my spiritual teachers during my life?

T he journey in between who you once were and who you are now becoming is where the dance of life really takes place.

—BARBARA DE ANGELIS

FOR THE WEEK AHEAD:

At the end of each day, for a week, take a few minutes to reflect on times you experienced God's presence.

We are not human beings on a spiritual journey; we are spiritual beings on a human journey.

—STEPHEN COVEY

9

The Gift of Enough

On the sixth day they gathered twice as much food, two omers apiece. When all the leaders of the congregation came and told Moses, he said to them, "This is what the LORD has commanded: 'Tomorrow is a day of solemn rest, a holy sabbath to the LORD; bake what you want to bake and boil what you want to boil, and all that is left over put aside to be kept until morning.'" So they put it aside until morning, as Moses commanded them; and it did not become foul, and there were no worms in it. Moses said, "Eat it today, for today is a sabbath to the LORD; today you will not find it in the field. Six days you shall gather it; but on the seventh day, which is a sabbath, there will be none." On the seventh day some of the people went out to gather, and they found none. The LORD said to Moses, "How long will you refuse to keep my commandments and instructions? See! The LORD has given you the sabbath, therefore on the sixth day he gives you food for two days; each of you stay where you are; do not leave your place on the seventh day." So the people rested on the seventh day.

—Ex 16:22-30

For the Jews, the miracle of manna paralleled the miracle of creation. It showed God's intimate involvement in the world. This was not an absent God. For forty years in the desert God fed approximately three million people. Each morning, manna, a sweet honey bread wafer, fell from the sky for the people to eat. God gave them just enough for each day. If they gathered more than they could eat in one day, the leftover manna would be full of worms the next day. If they were lazy and did not gather the manna provided, it would melt. God provided for them on a daily basis. They had to trust God to give them enough to eat, enough of everything they needed.

On the sixth day God gave two days' worth of manna so there would be no gathering on the Sabbath. They did not have to work for their food on the Sabbath even if the work was only to gather the manna from the ground and carry it to their tents. But many did not trust God and tried to be in control by overconsuming or hoarding. Those who ate too much went hungry on the Sabbath, while those who gathered more than they needed during the week in an effort to hoard were disappointed to find that their stores of manna were rotten.

Exodus tells us that the Israelites wandered in the desert on a journey to the Promised Land. All their possessions had to be carried; those who could carry more possessed more. Carrying equaled ownership and security. The very first activity restricted by Sabbath law was carrying. On the Sabbath the people could not carry anything. They had to lay down the symbols of ownership and security. The restriction against carrying also made it impractical to travel or make progress on their journey because they would have to leave their possessions behind. With that one restriction, God ensured that on the Sabbath the people would recognize that their possessions, security, and achievement were dependent on God.

Making things, producing, harvesting, and trading were all restricted so that the Sabbath would be solely about God's presence. Breaking the Sabbath in spirit or in fact was the central concern of most of the prophets. Nehemiah, Isaiah, Ezekiel, and Amos explicitly warned against breaking the Sabbath and equated the people's adherence to the Sabbath with their loyalty to God. The prophets were concerned about the people who overlooked their relationship with God in favor of their economic gain.

The New Testament also reminds us of the dangers of hoarding and overconsuming instead of attending to God and his people. Both Luke and Matthew recount the story of the rich man who doesn't notice the starving Lazarus at his doorstep. When the rich man dies, instead of living out eternity in luxury, he is destined to be in eternal torment because of this neglect. All the evangelists warn against feeling secure from having plentiful possessions, like barns full of food. Instead, the writers tell us of a generous God who will certainly care for us even more than he does for the lilies of the field and the birds of the sky. I hope that I don't ignore those in need like the rich man ignored Lazarus. But if my doorstep is the whole world, how could I ever give enough?

My husband and I have talked about how much we need to save for retirement and our children's college funds. We feel a sense of responsibility to save so that we can help our children and avoid becoming a burden to others. We have been conflicted about how much we can give to someone who needs help now, versus our responsibility to save for the future. I'm not sure what it would mean to follow the apostles' command to trust completely in God for all of my needs, but I do know that it's worth asking the questions. Learning to trust in God's security reminds me that I shouldn't be dependent on the government's economic system or my own power. If I believe that I am the master of my universe, or if I put my trust in the government's economic and political systems, I will be vulnerable to events that could make me economically, emotionally, or physically poor.

I wonder if those who lived in the past, when life was physically more difficult, might have actually had an advantage. They looked forward to their "reward in heaven." Just finishing their hard life was reward enough for some. They didn't have any illusions about being in control of their fate, so they could concentrate on the few things that were in their control.

Now, many of us have so many choices. Having greater means is good, but maybe the power to choose has become an illusion. It's easy to think that because we have more choices we have control over life and death and our circumstances. But cancer doesn't know that you have a very important job or enough money and power to pay for the best of everything. When a mother delivers a premature infant who will likely have lifelong struggles, all the money and power in the world can't bring back the dream of a perfectly healthy child.

In modern biblical commentaries, the word "money" is often substituted for the word "manna" to help us understand the parallels between the Hebrews of old and us today. It wasn't that long ago that the Sabbath restrictions were written into our own laws. I remember the "blue laws" that restricted commerce on Sundays. They have largely disappeared from the United States and many Christians don't even realize that those laws were in place to protect the Sabbath.

Chad Myers, in his book *Sabbath Economics,* said that the economic implications of the Bible (especially the practice of Sabbath) could be summarized by three axioms:

- the world as created by God is abundant, with enough for everyone—provided that human communities restrain their appetites and live within limits;
- disparities in wealth and power are not natural, but the result of human sin;
- the prophetic message calls people to the practice of redistribution.

These axioms imply that living with enough and giving away excess can be not only an act of charity but also an act of God's justice. When some of us live with excess there is only enough for a few. When all of us live with enough, God provides enough for all. Statistics report that the wealthiest 20 percent of the world's population control more than 80 percent of the world's wealth while the lowest 20 percent control only 2 percent of the wealth.

The disparity between rich and poor today is no better than the disparity between the Pharaohs and the Israelites in ages past. The Hebrew prophets were messengers of God who called the people to live by God's justice. They were not well liked because the action required to bring justice usually involved some personal sacrifice. It was probably one of the prophets who started the saying: "Don't blame the messenger!" John the Baptist was one of those prophets; he told his followers, "Whoever has two coats must share with anyone who has none . . ." (Lk 3:11). I read somewhere an updated practical version of that same command which said, "If you have two coats in your closet, then you have someone else's coat in your closet."

Compliance to Sabbath was an act of obedience and trust. The Israelites had to trust that God would provide enough for them each day, including the day when they did not work for it. Monks of all major religions, now and in the past, have begged for their daily sustenance as an act of voluntary poverty and as a discipline of trusting in God. The Japanese name for the monk's begging bowl is *oryoki,* which means "just enough." Jesus told his disciples to carry no walking stick, no food or money, and to depend on the kindness of strangers. The disciples were to trust that God would provide enough and then be obedient to God by accepting that what was provided was enough.

Saint Francis of Assisi took Jesus' command literally and made it the foundation of his order. Francis and his brothers wore a rope around their waist to show that they did not have a money belt or wallet. They, like the Israelites, did not carry anything so that their security, dignity, and identity were not based on what they possessed. Their security was grounded in a relationship with the Father, not in the social or political system. They were living examples of Sabbath. How countercultural that would be today!

Our society is quite the opposite—"There is no such thing as enough." If you have one, two is better. Bigger is better. More is better. Shopping must be available twenty-four hours a day, seven days a week—we can't seem to get enough. The underlying cultural message today is that if I *have* more then I *am* more. If I acquire enough then I am enough; but enough for whom? God's message is that I am already enough for him; he made me and that is enough.

While I was writing this chapter I took a break to read my e-mail and found an Internet story forwarded to me by a friend. I typically don't open those e-mail chain letters but I had to stop and read this one. The subject line read, "I wish you enough." The story went like this:

> Recently I overheard a mother and daughter in their last moments together at the airport. They had announced the departure. Standing near the security gate, they hugged and the mother said, "I love you and I wish you enough."

> The daughter replied, "Mom, our life together has been more than enough; your love is all I ever needed. I wish you enough, too, Mom." They kissed and the daughter left. The mother walked over and sat next to me, with tears in her eyes. I tried not to intrude on her privacy but she welcomed me in by asking, "Did you ever say good-bye to someone knowing it would be forever?"

> "Yes, I have," I replied. "Forgive me for asking, but why is this good-bye forever?"

> "I am old and she lives so far away. I have challenges ahead and the reality is—the next trip back will be for my funeral," she said.

I had to ask: "When you were saying good-
bye, I heard you say 'I wish you enough.'
May I ask what that means?"

She began to smile. "That's a wish that has
been handed down from other generations. My
parents used to say it to everyone." She paused
a moment and looked up, remembering it in
detail, and she smiled even more. Then, turning
toward me she shared the following: "I wish
you enough sun to keep your attitude bright. I
wish you enough rain to appreciate the sun
more. I wish you enough happiness to keep
your spirit alive. I wish you enough pain so that
the smallest joys in life appear much bigger. I
wish you enough gain to satisfy your wanting. I
wish you enough loss to appreciate all that you
possess. I wish you enough hellos to get you
through the final good-bye."

It will probably take a lifetime for me to realize the
foundational belief of enough and then to act out of that
belief. Sabbath is a time for me to stop acquiring and building
and to look around and see that I have enough and that I am
enough. Sabbath teaches "enough!"

The ability to simplify means to
eliminate the unnecessary so that
the necessary may speak.

—HANS HOFMANN

For Meditation:
- Where in my life is there excess?
- What would it mean for me to trust that God will provide?
- Do I believe that I am enough for God? Why or why not?

For Discussion or Journaling:
Think of a time when you had to strip away something in your life and get to the bare bones. How did that feel? What insights did it bring to you?

For the Week Ahead:
Before you buy something, ask yourself if you already have enough or if this will add something important to your life. Put aside a day this week when you will not buy or sell anything.

As for those who in the present age are rich, command them not to be haughty, or to set their hopes on the uncertainty of riches, but rather on God who richly provides us with everything for our enjoyment.

—1 TIMOTHY 6:17

10

Jesus and the Sabbath

Again he entered the synagogue, and a man was there who had a withered hand. They watched him to see whether he would cure him on the sabbath, so that they might accuse him. And he said to the man who had the withered hand, "Come forward." Then he said to them, "Is it lawful to do good or to do harm on the sabbath, to save life or to kill?" But they were silent. He looked around at them with anger; he was grieved at their hardness of heart and said to the man, "Stretch out your hand." He stretched it out, and his hand was restored.

—MARK 3:1–5

If the Sabbath was a foundational principle of Judaism, why did Jesus seemingly go out of his way to break the Sabbath? All of the gospels report a number of occasions when Jesus broke the Sabbath. I think he used each episode to show a deeper meaning of Sabbath. Jesus healed and fed the hungry on the Sabbath to show his obedience to God's true will, that the greatest gift of Sabbath is a loving relationship with God and his people.

On the Sabbath, Jesus entered the synagogue in his hometown and read from scripture. He chose the passage from Isaiah that said, "The spirit of the Lord GOD is upon me, because the LORD has anointed me; he has sent me to bring good news to the oppressed, to bind up the brokenhearted, to proclaim liberty to the captives, and release to the prisoners; to proclaim the year of the Lord's favor . . ." (Is 61:1–2). Luke's gospel says that the people were amazed as Jesus went on to say, "Today this scripture has been fulfilled in your hearing" (Lk 4:21).

Jesus saw his mission as freeing the captives—bringing about God's justice. Sabbath, too, was about freedom from oppression. The Jews had endured life under Babylonian, Egyptian, and now Roman rulers; all were oppressors. The Sabbath gave slaves and even animals a day to rest, a day of freedom. It was a day set apart to be different from the other six days of work and oppression. Deuteronomy 5:15 says: "Remember that you were a slave in the land of Egypt, and the LORD your God brought you out from there with a mighty hand and an outstretched arm; therefore the LORD your God commanded you to keep the sabbath day." The Sabbath was a reminder that they were freed from oppression by the grace of God.

The Jewish culture of the first century viewed those with riches as people blessed by God. The poor were those who were not blessed or favored by God; therefore, they must be sinners. Those with a mental or physical illness or defect were also considered sinners. Their poverty or infirmity was justification for separating them from society, labeling them as people condemned by God. But Jesus' self-proclaimed mission was to bring good news to the poor, to heal the infirm, and to bring freedom to all. When Jesus broke the Sabbath, he did so to restore people's dignity, freeing them from their state as outcasts. Jesus freed them to be reunited with the society. He healed the man with the withered hand which, in the Jewish mind, restored him to a place of favor with God. On another Sabbath in Luke's gospel (13:10–16), he tells of Jesus healing a woman who is possessed. Jesus heals her with the words, "Woman you are free of your infirmity." She stands up and starts thanking God, but Jesus is again reprimanded by the religious authorities for healing on the Sabbath. He responds to their complaints, saying, "You hypocrites! Which of you does not let his ox or ass out of the stall on the Sabbath to water it? Should not this daughter of Abraham here, who has been in the bondage of Satan for eighteen years, have been released from her shackles on the Sabbath?" By healing the woman, Jesus restores her dignity as a daughter of Abraham. He restores her to her rightful place in the community.

John's gospel gives insight into Jesus' message about the Sabbath and also reports times when Jesus healed on the Sabbath. Similar to the other gospel accounts, the religious authorities condemned him for breaking the Sabbath rules. But this time, the scriptures go on to say that they began planning to kill Jesus. It seems a little extreme to want to kill someone for doing good work on the Sabbath. John explains, "For this reason the Jews were seeking all the more to kill him, because he was not only breaking the sabbath, but was also calling God his own Father, thereby making himself equal to God"(Jn 5:18). They were driven to thoughts of murder because Jesus kept proclaiming his intimate relationship with God.

When Jesus healed a person, he clarified his action, saying, "My Father is still working, and I also am working" (Jn 5:17).

By working on the Sabbath, Jesus claimed his sonship. In the same gospel, Jesus again explained the relationship: "Very truly, I tell you, the Son can do nothing on his own, but only what he sees the Father doing. . . . The Father loves the Son and shows him all that he himself is doing . . ." (Jn 5:19–20).

Although Jesus always pointed beyond himself to God, he lived out of his relationship with God and that was something new. It was a threat to the established image of a God who spoke to his people through a prophet or through the church. Jesus spoke with authority not given by the establishment but directly from God. Jesus broke the Sabbath because he acted, not in obedience to the law, but in obedience to his Father.

In each case, Jesus broke the Sabbath laws to feed or heal someone. In each case, Jesus cared for and loved his neighbor. The Pharisees, representing the conventional wisdom of the day, reproached Jesus for breaking their most sacred law, but Jesus pointed out that there is a greater law that must be obeyed. It is the law of relationship, on which Sabbath itself is based. In Matthew's gospel, Jesus had an encounter with the Pharisees where he stated that law clearly:

> "Teacher, which commandment in the law is the greatest?" He said to him, " 'You shall love the Lord your God with all your heart, and with all your soul, and with all your mind.' This is the greatest and first commandment. And a second is like it: 'You shall love your neighbor as yourself.' On these two commandments hang all the law and the prophets" (Mt 22:36–40).

The first commandment is the greatest because it establishes the primacy of our relationship with God. The second restates the first when it says that our relationship with others should be like our relationship with God. The second command reflects the first because God lives in relationships of love. I am capable of love because God loves in me. The divine in me recognizes and loves the divine spark in my neighbor. When I love my neighbor and myself, I recognize and love God.

Jesus said that all laws are based on these commandments that establish our relationships. The Sabbath laws, likewise, are based on these first two commandments. Jesus did not argue about the correctness of keeping the Sabbath; instead he pointed out the intent of the law. Jesus broke the *law* of the Sabbath in order to fulfill the *spirit* of the Sabbath, the underlying law of relationship. Jesus wasn't putting personal gain or image above the Sabbath law. He was fulfilling the Sabbath law which, still today, calls us into loving relationship with God and our neighbors.

I see Jesus' breaking of the Sabbath as a living parable. The parables were stories Jesus told that seemed to have an obvious ending but that actually ended with a twist. The stories challenged the standard assumptions and values of the day. An example of a parable story is "The Good Samaritan." The crowd expected that in a story about the beaten man being saved, the savior would be a Jewish priest or a Levite, the natural heroes of the day. Instead, in Jesus' story, the hero who saved the life of the beaten man was a Samaritan, someone who in that day was thought to be evil and untouchable. Jesus lived out the same parable paradox when he healed on the Sabbath.

In a religious society, like that of Palestine in the first century, the good people followed the religious rules. Then along came Jesus, who was master, rabbi, teacher, and messiah, breaking the religious rules. The good guy was the rule-breaker. Jesus challenged his fellow Jews to look at the laws differently, just as he challenges us to do today. He pointed out that the law can become an idol if we don't look deeper to the intent of the law. Even the Sabbath can become an idol, if we lose sight of the one who commanded the Sabbath. It was and is a warning against idolizing the *practice* instead of the *relationship*. Sabbath is the path of relationship, but it is not the relationship itself.

Jews of his day, at least those Jesus criticized, were bound by legalism. They idolized the law, instead of using the law to deepen their contact with God and spread his justice to all. They needed to break from their cultural assumptions. Jesus asked them to step back and look at what a relationship with God really meant. They idolized the law, and so Jesus broke the law to force them to look at their cultural assumptions and reestablish God above all things (including the law). Jesus broke the Sabbath to force them to choose between the Sabbath regulations and the loving relationship with God through others. Jesus chose love.

In Jesus' community, the religious laws had become oppressive for many who were sick or poor. In the spirit of Moses, Jesus offered them freedom. Jews were to remember on the Sabbath that they, too, were once slaves, released from their bondage by the grace of God. Jesus healed on the Sabbath to bring freedom, which should have reminded the people of the true meaning of Sabbath. Jesus broke from the legalism of society to practice the essence of Sabbath. Legalism may be an idol or false god for some of us, as it was for the Pharisees, but certainly our culture has many more "isms" that may be our false gods: materialism, individualism, consumerism, militarism, and nationalism, to name a few. Jesus continues to challenge us to look at our assumptions and values and to determine who God really is.

A few years ago, I was a member of a group in our parish that looked at the social teachings of Jesus. All of us were active members of the church and the community, but we took time out for a year to do extensive reading, hours of discussion each week, and ministry work, specifically to learn more about these social teachings. The program was called "JustFaith." During the buildup to the Gulf War, we studied the nonviolent teachings of Jesus. One in our group was a thirty-year veteran of the Air Force and many others had family and friends in the military. All of us felt like we were good Americans and Christians. It was very difficult to try to assimilate the nonviolent teaching of Jesus with our desire to believe in our country and government. Most of us were very conflicted. I realized, then, that Jesus almost never makes me feel comfortable in my beliefs. Much more often he makes me rethink my assumptions and my values.

Noone of these forms of engagement in personal and political transformation, however, can be sustained or deepened without the central spiritual discipline of Sabbath keeping.

—CHAD MYERS,
SABBATH ECONOMICS

FOR MEDITATION:

- What are my cultural assumptions? Cultural sayings or clichés are a clue to the assumptions. For example, there are assumptions contained in the following clichés:

    People should pull themselves up by
    their boot straps.
    If you work hard you will succeed.
    Money talks.
    Knowledge is power.

- What would cause me to rethink my assumptions?
- What are my false idols?

FOR DISCUSSION OR JOURNALING:
- What is Jesus saying to me about the Sabbath?
- Why do I do ministry? Is God really calling me to the ministries I have chosen or am I being called to something else?

There is a pervasive form of contemporary violence . . . activism and overwork. To allow oneself to be carried away by a multitude of conflicting concerns, to surrender to too many demands, to commit oneself to too many projects, to want to help everyone in everything, is to succumb to violence. . . . It destroys the fruitfulness of our own work, because it kills the root of inner wisdom which makes work fruitful.

—THOMAS MERTON

11

The Rituals of Sabbath

When I was in elementary school, I had a good friend named Jennifer. She and her family were Orthodox Jews. I would sometimes go home with her after school on Friday to spend the night.

Her house was always full of friends and relatives. I remember wonderful smells from food and candles. The table was filled with plates and bowls of food. There were plates of sliced meats and bowls filled with pasta rolls and things I'd never seen before. There was a whole side table full of candy and sweet breads and muffins. We must have eaten a dozen times in the next twenty-four hour period.

Before dinner on Friday, we went downstairs and her mom sang a blessing in a language that I didn't understand and lit two tall, white candles. I remember her mom motioning in the air above the candles like she was pulling the smoke toward her face. We ate at a big dining room table as they took turns telling family stories. Then different members of the family said what I assumed were prayers and they all sang songs. Afterward, the kids were allowed to go play while the adults sat around the table, sipped wine or coffee, and talked until it was very late. We were all called back at bedtime to pray and eat again.

In the morning, we repeated the ritual. We got up and dressed, then ate again before going to the synagogue. Breakfast was a special treat for me, because Catholics weren't allowed to eat or drink until after Mass. The day was full of praying, eating, and playing. It was a wonderful day, even though I didn't understand most of what was happening. The language was strange to me and the food was unfamiliar, but who could complain? It was like a party every week! The first time I spent Sabbath with them I thought it was someone's birthday or a holiday. I couldn't believe that they celebrated like that every week!

I would never describe my family as one that kept the Sabbath, but when I think about it, our Sunday traditions weren't so different. It was much simpler and quieter. We didn't have as many guests as my friend's family, but then again we had a full house with just the twelve of us. We got up early and went to Mass, then went directly to the bakery to get donuts on our way home.

Wherever we lived we found a bakery with homemade donuts. They had to be crunchy on the outside but warm and soft on the inside, and the coffee cake had to have a thick layer of cinnamon and sugar crust on the top. It was important to get to the bakery early to get the best selection of donuts. We would buy a whole rack of the glazed and chocolate-covered ones, as well as a couple of coffee cakes and a few loaves of fresh bread for sandwiches later. I pitied the families who came after us because my siblings and I consumed an impressive amount of donuts. There would only be a couple of stray jelly-filled or coconut-covered donuts remaining after we left the bakery.

At home we were allowed to have as many donuts and pieces of coffee cake as we wanted. Then we spent a leisurely afternoon watching old movies, reading, or playing a board game called "Wahoo." It was family time, but our friends were always welcome. The best thing about it was that we didn't have to clean the house or do yard work. We didn't need an excuse to sit around and just be lazy. In our family, that was a day different from all other days.

Exploring the roots of Sabbath has given me a better appreciation of its rituals and practices. I found that the ancient Hebrews, modern Jews, and Christians have some common Sabbath traditions. The common traditions involve building relationships within the family and the larger faith community. These faiths share the components of communal worship and individual prayer. If my Catholic family and my friend's Jewish family are any indication, it would seem that sharing meals is a necessary element of the ritual. As a part of these traditions, I feel a special need to imitate the ancient people of God by taking a radical step back from my culture, to do something or not do something so that the Sabbath day is very different from every other day.

Sabbath is about relationships with others. I am so grateful for my family and friends that it only seems right to take a few moments to recognize them as God's blessings. I also try to invest time and energy in those relationships. During the week I try to stop and listen to a friend or take a walk with my son, but on the Sabbath I make a more conscious effort to take time to be with others. I try to call my parents and some of my siblings or old friends to reconnect with them. I have set a pattern for our Sundays, similar to the one my mother set for us. We do the chores on Saturday, so Sunday can be a day to relax. I know my children like Sundays, because I don't have a "to do" list for them. It's a good day to watch movies together or read a good book.

The weekend for my family would not be complete unless we attended Mass on Saturday evening or Sunday morning. Biblical scholar Eugene Peterson said, "Worship is the strategy by which we interrupt our preoccupation with ourselves and attend to the presence of God. Worship is the time and place that we assign for deliberate attentiveness to God . . . not because he's confined to time and place but because our self-importance is so insidiously relentless that if we don't deliberately interrupt ourselves regularly we have no chance of attending to him at all at other times and in other places." Peterson's description of worship correlates well with the principles of Sabbath. Sabbath interrupts our repetition of doing and gives us the opportunity to join with others in praise of God.

My family is lucky to have a worship service that is truly a celebration of God's presence in our community. After Mass we socialize over coffee and treats for the kids. Our parish is like an extended family. It is filled with so many people we have come to love. My parish has shown me, time and again, that a community founded in faith and grounded in the spirit is not only possible, but is also inevitable when there is a gathering of people who listen to God and serve others.

Another important part of our Sabbath is a meal with family and sometimes friends. The cooking doesn't need to be fancy; in fact some of my favorite meals have been the simplest ones, especially during snowstorms. In Virginia, we don't get much snow, so a few inches will shut down the city. The snow usually melts before we ever see a snow plow in our neighborhood, but while the snow is still on the roads we can't go anywhere, so we enjoy sledding or staying warm inside.

For many years we had good friends who lived in the house next door. Whenever we were snowed in, Julie and I would throw together a meal with whatever we could find. We sat around drinking steaming hot chocolate, watching our kids play in the snow. When they finally got soaked to the bone, they came in and we would raid the cupboards for chips and salsa, chicken soup, chili, and hot dogs with macaroni and cheese. None of it went together but it was perfectly wonderful for us. Neither Julie nor I liked the cold very much, but we both looked forward to those snow days.

In my role as a therapist working with people who have difficulty swallowing, I see every day how *not* being able to share a meal affects my patients and their families. I've learned that sharing a meal is more than just a physiologic event. It is a psychological, social, and spiritual experience.

It was no accident that Jesus so often used the meal as a metaphor for God's unconditional love and his kingdom. The early church, moved by the spirit, made the eucharistic meal the central symbol of their relationship with God and with each other. Sharing meals together has been important throughout history and across cultures. To eat together is to be intimate and vulnerable to one another. Sharing a meal is the deepest and most universal sign of unity. Sabbath is an opportunity to share a meal. It's an opportunity to deepen our relationships with family and friends and to be grateful for the God that makes it all possible.

One thing that my family had never done on Sunday was to make a conscious effort to step back from ordinary daily life. If we needed something we went to the store to get it. If we had a project due in school we worked on Sunday until it was finished. There was nothing about Sunday that significantly interfered with our daily lives.

But the practice of Sabbath does take some sacrifices. A discipline of keeping the Sabbath would mean that if we ran out of milk on the Sabbath then we would go without milk. I would need to plan any work or chores so they were done before the Sabbath or they would have to wait. I couldn't paint the bathroom and my husband couldn't fix the car. We would have to commit to another way of life for that day. But that different way of life is one of the primary gifts of practicing Sabbath. For a day or even a few hours Sabbath allows me to leave the rat race for a while.

In the world today, being busy has become a virtue. I feel guilty if my husband comes home and I'm not doing something productive. When I ask someone how her day has been, I expect her to tell me how busy it was. Sabbath has given me permission to rest physically and mentally. It has given me permission to say "no" to just one more obligation. Sabbath has given me permission to stop being busy. It gives me time to look at my choices, my actions, and my world with new eyes. It is a time to question the things I do every other day without question.

Sabbath rest can mean different things to different people. It can be twenty-four or four hours. It can be daily, weekly, or monthly. The important thing is to take the time. For the ancient Hebrews it was a time to break the cycle of physical labor and allow for rest. For me and many others today, work is not particularly active, so physical rest is not a break in the cycle of days. I need a mental rest. I need a period of time to stop planning, stop problem solving, stop searching for answers.

Today, as an adult, the best way for me to rejuvenate with Sabbath is to sit in the sun and feel the breeze on my face or read a good book in front of the fireplace. For others, it might be to take a leisurely walk or bike ride. The activity itself is not as important as how it is done: walk, ride, read, or sit and stare at the clouds with an attitude of prayer. Do everything that day with particular attention to God's action in your life.

Rabbi Lawrence Kushner talks about God becoming present to Moses through the burning bush in his book *Jewish Spirituality*. He points out that God chose to come in a relatively small miracle, because it required Moses to stop and pay attention to the fact that the bush was not consumed, even though it was on fire. Only when Moses paused and paid attention could God then speak to him.

I, too, want to be attuned to the smallest indication of God's presence in nature, in others, and in myself. I want to do or not do with the intention of getting to know God and myself better. I don't want it to be a time to numb out or withdraw. I don't want to do anything that will decrease my awareness or sensitivity. Instead, I want to practice a different kind of attention. I want to practice an attention to the inner self, to develop an increased awareness of who I am and what I am called to be.

Sabbath is a time to explore different types of prayer, to get to know God through scripture and to look for him in unexpected places and people. It is a time to ask the bigger questions. I was not converted at one moment; my life has been full of little conversions. The culture has such a pull on me that I need to step away from it regularly and allow God to convert me again and again.

I believe what Jesus said in John's gospel: "The Advocate, the Holy Spirit, whom the Father will send in my name, will teach you everything, and remind you of all that I have said to you" (Jn 14:26). Sabbath is a time for me to open my heart and ready my soul to listen to the spirit. My siblings and I spent many hours planting flowers around the many houses where we lived. Our father often told us that the preparation of the soil is the most important part of gardening. Sabbath prepares the soil of my soul. Sabbath stirs up the dirt, sifts out the junk, and helps me dig deep so I can plant the seeds of faith. Then Sabbath teaches me to slow the pace; to watch attentively and wait patiently for the movement of God. Sabbath teaches me to be still so I can know my God. At the definitive moment when I meet God, I wonder, will I recognize him, will I know him, and will I have anything in common with him? The only way to answer "yes" to those questions is to start asking them now. Sabbath gives me a discipline to explore and allows me to develop a relationship with God here and now.

SABBATH RITUALS:

Don't wear a watch.
Turn off the phones.
Learn about something new in the created world.
Share a simple meal with friends and/or family.
Explore a new type of prayer.
Read scripture.
Establish a tradition with your friends and/or family.

FOR MEDITATION
- Do I feel a need for Sabbath?
- What does the concept of rest mean to me?

FOR DISCUSSION OR JOURNALING:
How can I re-create Sabbath in my life?

Just sit there right now, don't do a thing, just rest, for your separation from God is the hardest work in the world.

—HAFIZ

(FOURTEENTH-CENTURY MYSTIC)

12

Accepting the Gifts of Sabbath

Observe the sabbath day and keep it holy, as the LORD your God commanded you. Six days you shall labor and do all your work. But the seventh day is a sabbath to the LORD your God; you shall not do any work—you, or your son or your daughter, or your male or female slave, or your ox or your donkey, or any of your livestock, or the resident alien in your towns, so that your male and female slave may rest as well as you. Remember that you were a slave in the land of Egypt, and the LORD your God brought you out from there with a mighty hand and an outstretched arm; therefore the LORD your God commanded you to keep the sabbath day.

—DEUTERONOMY 5:12–15

It seems presumptuous of me to just ignore the third commandment. I don't just ignore any other commandment. On a bad day I might try to justify lying or coveting but I still know it's wrong. Why then does it seem all right to ignore the Sabbath? It is often the commandment that is "out of sight, out of mind." Does that mean, then, that a relationship with God is also "out of sight, out of mind," easy to ignore? Even before the Ten Commandments were given to Moses, God instituted the Sabbath. The first few verses of Genesis say that God declared the seventh day as holy. God sanctified the Sabbath, making it a special time set apart. He instituted a Sabbath, a holy day of rest. He didn't have to teach us or remind us how to work. It seems we do that by default.

My son brought home the classroom pet many years ago. It was a hamster and in its cage was an exercise wheel. That hamster ran on his wheel for hours. I often wondered if he really liked the motion or if he kept running just because he didn't know how to get off the wheel. Sometimes I feel like that in my own life. I keep doing and doing, most times with purpose, but too often I'm just moving because I don't know how to slow down or I think the world might fall apart if I do slow down. But God has given us permission to slow down. More than that, he has commanded that we get off the wheel periodically, not only for rest, but, more important, so we can recognize that we are cared for and loved.

Sabbath allows me the room to step back from the world and reestablish that I belong to God. The Sabbath rest isn't just a short vacation. When I go on vacation I am fatigued from planning, packing, and preparing. While on vacation I take part in many different activities to have fun with my family. Then, I come home to laundry, cleaning, and preparing myself for work and the kids for school. It's exhausting. The problem is that the goal of our vacation is to do fun things with the family. The goal of Sabbath is different.

Sabbath is an intentional, radical kind of rest. Sabbath is an intentional break from the ordinary. It's a resting of the mind, body, and spirit. It's a reconnecting with the self and a resting in God.

> And on the seventh day God finished the work
> that he had done, and he rested on the seventh
> day from all the work that he had done. So
> God blessed the seventh day and hallowed it
> (Gn 2:2–3).

God blessed the seventh day and made it holy because on that day he rested from all the work he had done in creation. The Jewish Midrash (a classic book of interpretation of scripture and tradition) says: "On the Sabbath, God created rest." The seventh day was holy because God *created* rest. The seventh day wasn't holy because God desperately needed and deserved a break. Sabbath rest was so vital and necessary to us that God created it and proclaimed it holy.

The importance of the Sabbath rest is shown over and over again in scripture. While praying with these scriptures I was struck by two things—first, keeping the Sabbath was a commandment, and, second, it was given as a gift. Initially, those two things seemed contradictory to me. How could you have a gift that you must accept under pain of death? Scripture suggests the death penalty for those who violate the Sabbath. As I studied these scriptures I realized that these two things are consistent.

First, the gift: The Jewish teacher, Michael Berg, described the Sabbath, saying, "The creator has given us many gifts, but the sages say none greater than the gift of Sabbath." Scripture tells us the gift of Sabbath is an integral part of the covenant God established with his people. Exodus 31:16–17 says: "Therefore the Israelites shall keep the sabbath, observing the sabbath throughout their generations, as a perpetual covenant. It is a sign forever between me and the people of Israel. . . ." Sabbath is the gift of relationship with God—the ultimate gift. This gift is not just a casual gesture; it is a covenant and an everlasting bond. Even if we try to dismiss or negate God, God overwhelms us with his love. He does not release us from the covenant.

God fed his wandering horde of people for forty years in the desert, showing them that he was not an absent God. He was daily in their midst taking care of them. Sabbath was sign and symbol of that bond, that presence in their lives. It was the sign of the covenant of love between God and his beloved. Sabbath is the ever-present reminder of the ever-present God.

Now, the hook: Sabbath was also mandated. It was given as a command instead of a suggestion or request because practicing Sabbath eliminates other idols. It puts our priorities back in order. The Kabbalah teaches that those who do not keep the Sabbath are idol worshipers. Genesis says that God gave man dominion over the earth for six days, but on the seventh day humans must rest. On the seventh day, man cannot do for himself; he must remember who gave the gift of creation. Sabbath reminds us that there is but one God. Without that perpetual reminder we would undoubtedly idolize ourselves, someone, or something else. We would start to feel in control. We could be seduced by the illusion that we are the masters of our universe. It is a great burden to be your own god and an unfair burden to idolize someone else.

I remember a friend who came to me with some marital issues. She told me that her husband didn't understand that her child was the center of her universe. It was her conviction that literally everything had to revolve around the child. I'm sure I surprised her when I said that I hoped her child didn't think he was the center of her universe because that was too much responsibility for anyone, especially a child. We were made in God's image to be in relationship with him, to share in his creative work, but not to take his place.

When we idolize something or someone other than God we are out of relationship with him. So the other side of this gift is the reality that without it there is spiritual death. The death penalty of the Hebrew scriptures for those who did not keep the Sabbath didn't have to be an imposed physical death—the scripture was merely stating the facts: without Sabbath, the covenant relationship with God, there is spiritual death. That is why Sabbath is one of the three major tenants of Judaism and why it should also be pivotal in our lives.

In his book *The Sabbath*, Abraham Heschel wrote: "Judaism is a religion of time aiming at the sanctification of time. Judaism teaches us to be attached to holiness in time, to be attached to sacred events. . . . The Sabbaths are our great cathedrals." Time is a gift given to us all. The wealthy and powerful, the poor and weak, all have the same twenty-four hours in a day and 168 hours in a week. Time is the great equalizer. God gave us each the same gift of time; all we can do is decide what we'll do with it. Each moment that passes is given meaning because God sanctifies it. I can live in grace with the recognition that my life is time sanctified by God, but I can only do this if I am in relationship with him. He commanded me to live in relationship and he gave me a vehicle to develop and maintain that relationship. When God gave me free will he gave up some of his power. So for six days I act in his image by having power over the land, the animals, the water, and the sky. I live my life with the idea that I am in control. In Sabbath each week I am reminded that my power is limited, that I am only a steward of my world. Each week I am asked to reorient myself and remember that I am created, not creator. It seems such a little thing to ask.

Any long-term practice of Sabbath requires two things. First, I need a theology of Sabbath, which is a conviction that a relationship with God necessitates a regular, intentional stepping back from the world so that I might encounter God in new ways. I encounter God in the people and things of this world, but I need time and space to step back so I can observe, reflect, and recognize the many times during my day that God has been present. Second, I need a faith community to give support to the practice of Sabbath. Setting time aside when we are not working, producing, or consuming is so countercultural that I believe it would be difficult to practice Sabbath without a community of supporters and fellow travelers.

The Sabbath prompts me to ask, "To whom do I belong?" Six days a week I belong to a world where I compare myself to others; a world of working, achieving, possessing, and competing. When I belong to this world, I am caught up in judgments and determining who is worthy. Those are the rules of the cultural game, with human standards and values. Accordingly, if I follow the rules and do the right things, I am a success and deserve God's blessings. But that leaves man in control of God. Those are not God's rules.

Sabbath is a complete break from our set of rules and questions. During Sabbath I rest in God, in his mercy and love. Most of the week I am inundated with messages telling me to substantiate or prove my worthiness. At the very least, one day a week I can take time to hear the competing message of God.

Psychologists and advertisers will tell you that we believe and live by the messages we hear repeatedly. The Sabbath gives me time to concentrate, to listen to a different voice. It is time to allow God's ideals and values to have a chance to resonate. I need to get out of the secular consciousness and place myself into a different time and space. That is the holy place and time where I can look for God and allow God to find me. It is a place where God can catch me and I can be transformed. I need to break from the clutches of the culture and move into the arms of God. The world summons me to work, success, and achievement, and I believe God also summons me to work on behalf of others. But before God calls me to work or to service, he calls me to himself in Sabbath.

God's greatest gift is the gift of Sabbath, because it is the gift of time in his presence. When I was twenty-five my then-boyfriend and I shared dinner and the events of our day. We settled down to watch a favorite show on television. It was an evening like so many others, but he seemed nervous and anxious that night. All at once he put his arm around me and gave me a little black box. He waited with a huge smile on his face and hope in his eyes as I opened it. That box contained so much more than a ring. It contained his promise and mine to share our lives with each other. It was a gift that only came to fruition because it was accepted. Sabbath is that kind of gift. God waits patiently to offer us the gift of his presence, the gift of his creation, the gift of each moment, and so much more. He offers us the gift of himself and he delights in us when we accept.

Kathleen Casey received her B.S. in Speech Pathology and Audiology from James Madison University in Virginia in 1982 and her Masters in Speech Pathology from the University of Virginia in 1984. She is a Clinical Coordinator of Speech-Language Pathology at Henrico Doctors Hospital in Henrico, Virginia. She is also the author of Meal Stories. Kathleen is married to Thom and they have two children, Michele and Brian.

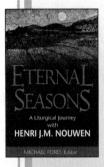

ETERNAL SEASONS
A Liturgical Journey With Henri J.M. Nouwen
EDITED BY MICHAEL FORD
Gathers for the first time selections for an entire liturgical year from forty of Nouwen's books. Features a thoughtful introduction for each of the liturgical season followed by a generous selection of brief passages.

ISBN: 1-893732-77-0 / 192 pages, hardcover / $18.95
Sorin Books

MAY I HAVE THIS DANCE?
JOYCE RUPP
A unique invitation to join with God in the dance of life, an invitation to experience God in the daily and seasonal rhythms of life. Explores twelve major themes, each one followed by prayer suggestions and other spiritual exercises.

ISBN: 0-87793-480-0 / 184 pages / $12.95
Ave Maria Press

MOMENT BY MOMENT
A Retreat in Everyday Life
CAROL ANN SMITH, SHCJ & EUGENE F. MERZ, SJ
Drawing on the classical retreat model, *The Spiritual Exercise of St. Ignatius*, **Moment by Moment** offers a new and inviting way to find God in our often busy and complex lives. Individuals or groups can use its simple format.

ISBN: 0-87793-945-4/ 96 pages / $12.95
Ave Maria Press
